The Accelerated Trainer

The Accelerated Trainer

Using Accelerated Learning Techniques to Revolutionize your Training

LEX McKEE

GOWER

Mind Maps® are a registered trademark of The Buzan Organization. Tony Buzan is the inventor of the process of Mind Mapping. For more information about Tony Buzan or the process of Mind Mapping, visit www.buzancentres.com.

Published by
Gower Publishing Limited
Gower House
Croft Road
Aldershot
Hants GU11 3HR
England

Gower Publishing Company
Suite 420
101 Cherry Street
Burlington, VT 05401-4405
USA

British Library Cataloguing in Publication Data

McKee, Lex
    The accelerated trainer : using accelerated learning
    techniques to revolutionize your training
    1. Employees – Training of 2. Educational acceleration
    I. Title
    658.3'124

ISBN: 0 566 08077 X

Library of Congress Control Number: 2003057011

Typeset by SetSystems Ltd, Saffron Walden, Essex
Printed and bound in Great Britain by MPG Books Ltd, Bodmin, Cornwall

Contents

List of Figures

First Words and Dedication

I wonder if, like me, you often bypass the Dedication to a book, yet, in this case, the dedication is a result of the dedication of others. I would like to share their dedication with you.

Two teachers modelled for me all that is good and precious about the vocation of teaching. This book is written in the hope that we all begin to realize what a power and a privilege we have in helping others realize their potential.

Most people have stories of exceptional teachers who stood out from the crowd. Perhaps the teacher had a distinctive style, a way of bringing the subject to life, of grounding it in our imagination – or in real life. This book has a story and a pedigree. The story begins with the vision and skill of two outstanding teachers whose transformational belief in my ability allowed me to become more fully myself. Their names are Barbara MacKeke and Joseph Rayner. To them I dedicate this book. I'm not sure Barbara knew the impact her passion and warmth had on her students, and I am not able to tell her now because she went on from this life many years ago. A tragic loss to us and to education. Fortunately, I have been able to express my thanks to Joe.

Joe and Barbara started the journey into education for me. Having helped me believe in myself through their extraordinary kindness, I wanted to be like them – to make a difference.

The Pedigree
There would be no book without those who have shared their insights with me: Tony Buzan and Vanda North (Mind Mapping), Colin Rose (Accelerated Learning), Howard Gardner (Multiple Intelligences), Daniel Goleman (Emotional Intelligence), John Grinder and Richard Bandler (Neurolinguistic programming), and all the participants who offered their own unique insights and feedback.

All good stories have a beginning, a middle and a rousing climax. In the middle of this story, the centre stage belongs to Tony Buzan and Vanda North, Chief Executive Officers of Buzan Centres. Anyone who has benefited from Mind Mapping will know that the thanks for this technique being widely available belongs to Tony and his brother Barry for inventing it, and to Vanda for spreading the good practice. Having worked closely with Vanda for years, and having had the privilege of magical times with both Vanda and Tony as friends and mentors, I have been fortunate enough to see my own knowledge and skill grow through the intervention of two of the best. They have watered the seed that Barbara and Joe planted.

In from the wings, watching and inspiring me has been perhaps the most influential man in bringing Accelerated Learning to a wider audience: Colin Rose. Colin has helped me clarify and refine my thinking and I am enormously grateful for his dedication and insights in the subject.

In the cast with me, over the 21 years we've been performing the show, have been my participants. Never have they been the audience, but rather players on the stage. I, too, have watched from the wings as so many of you have run and then taken flight with these transformational ideas. You have helped to keep me motivated and I thank you for your contributions that have helped refine and improve the model.

All good stories must have an ending, a rousing climax. I must thank my editor at Gower, Jonathan Norman, who has 'kept the faith' over the long gestation period of this project. This book has been written and rewritten, but never formally finished to our satisfaction. It has taken, once again, a visionary to help me 'finish the race' and win the prize of sharing these ideas with you. That visionary is my muse, my miracle worker, my catalyst, my favourite heroine – my Sandie. Thank you too for polishing this rough stone and for adding so many insights.

And finally, I must thank my sons who have often waited patiently for Dad to finish 'work' so that we can rejoice in the quality time we call 'play'. To Samuel, Joshua, and Richard I add my devotion and look forward to even better times ahead . . .

Lex McKee
March 2004
Worth Matravers, Dorset

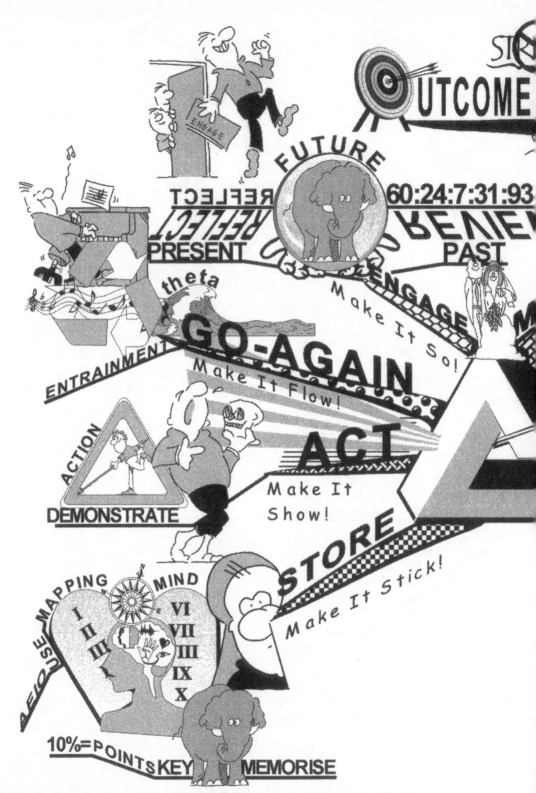

Figure 1 The overview of the M.E.S.S.A.G.E.™ model of Accelerated Training

© Lex McKee 09/07/01

Designed by Lex McKee: LexStudios@aol.com

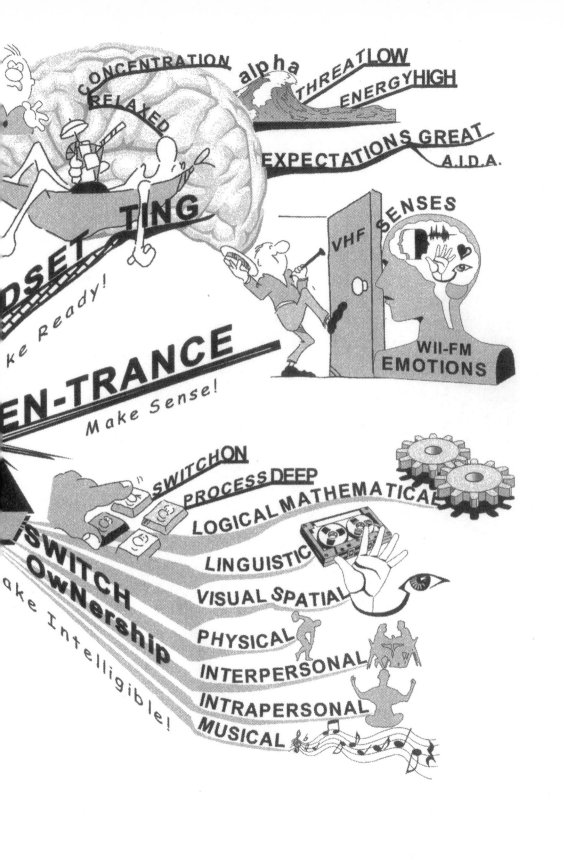

This is what Accelerated Learning is all about . . .

INTRODUCTION

The BIG Picture Overview

Our model for designing and delivering Accelerated Training is as refreshing and recreational as going on holiday. In fact, going on holiday is a great metaphor for describing the M.E.S.S.A.G.E.™ model of Accelerated Training.

Learning is both easy and enjoyable . . .

it is only undeveloped teaching styles that lead us to believe otherwise!

Learning is both easy and enjoyable. Ask anyone who has been consumed with a passion for their hobby. Memory recall is also easy. Ask anyone to recall the name of someone they are attracted to. In both cases, our *attention* is heightened and our motivation cranked up a gear because there is a key benefit for us from investing the energy it takes to assimilate and memorize new information. That learning and memorizing are both easy and enjoyable are core beliefs that drive our approach to learning, training and development. It is only our own self-imposed hang-ups and the undeveloped teaching styles we have encountered that have led us to believe otherwise.

Georgi Lozanov may legitimately be regarded as the founder of Accelerated Learning. He uses an approach called 'Suggestopaedia' which is largely focused on helping each learner remove their own *self-imposed* barriers to learning. Only in this way can they release their *reserve potential*.

Mindset
Entrance
Switch OwNership
Store
Act
Go-Again
Engage . . .
. . . a framework for the joy of
learning.

So, let us go on holiday. The model is a framework for a perfect holiday. M.E.S.S.A.G.E.™ is a mnemonic standing for Mindset (and mindsetting), Entrance, Switch OwNership, Store, Act, Go-Again, and Engage.

A perfect holiday begins well in advance. Months beforehand you gather a wide selection of brochures advertizing various destinations (or 'outcomes' in training terms). From these promotional materials you can get a picture of what might be different in your life depending on your choice of resort. This heightens the awareness of the tension between where you are now (for example, a cold, wet, foggy, dark Wednesday afternoon in central London) and where you could be if you commit to action (for example, a coral-white sandy beach by the Barrier Reef in Australia). If you are surfing the web for your desired destination, there may even be sound, video clips and perhaps a competition to entice you.

Joining instructions benefit from a little professional imagination – like a newspaper, radio show or TV documentary.

When was the last time you were invited to a workshop in such an enticing way? This is what the Mindset phase is all about – helping learners set realistically expanded expectations well in advance of the training and development event. We need to think holiday! We can send a brochure, a video, a CD-ROM, an invitation to our website – complete with competition! In our communication we can paint a sensory rich description of how each participant's life will be different as a result of this experience. We can create such a hunger that if we have to tell them we are fully booked, they will be screaming for a set of alternative dates.

Having a great journey really helps accentuate a positive Mindset!

Something that can really help a holiday get off to a magical start is to have a wonderful journey. How many times have you been on holiday or been to a workshop where you have had a dream journey – arriving early and refreshed? Probably not many. A key question for us as hosts to ask is, 'How can we help make the journey as smooth and pleasant as possible?' Good maps and parking instructions are clearly important, but, we can also

When we combine training with entertainment we get 'Entertrainment'® – a genre of communication that goes straight into long term memory, giving us higher return on investment.

begin to connect with the learners in advance by sending them a special tape or CD just for the journey – something we have kept in reserve for those last few hours before they arrive at our resort destination. Let us use some more imagination. I remember when the first training videos came out, so many 'talking heads'. Many audio programmes still suffer from 'talking head syndrome' – or perhaps 'sin-drone' – because it is a sin to make such boring broadcasts. The BBC would not get away with it so let us borrow their best practice. By way of strong contrast, I also remember the first 'Video Arts' productions with John Cleese. They were entertaining as well as training – an approach that we shall call 'Entertrainment'®. This is what we aspire to in our own programmes – advanced communications packages that entertain and inform so that each participant has a magnificent Mindset before entering the venue. There will be little need for ice breakers with such a warm-up.

When designing communications, think about producing a recording that is more like a radio show or a TV documentary. If the budget precludes a lavish production, then use that imagination (let us also remember that this approach is as much about getting YOU excited, interested and motivated as the delegates).

Imagine that you have now arrived at your holiday/training destination. This is what we will be calling 'Entrance' – the opener, the beginning of the 'live' experience. Here, our clients will want to check out that the resort is as good as the promotional materials and build up. They will move into a comparative phase, and will be looking for strong guidance and leadership from us as to the where, what, who, how and when of the promised recreational activities. This is where their senses are heightened because they want to experience *everything* and get their money's worth. They look here, there and everywhere to get the feel of the place and the pace. If we as hosts then provide a sensory rich experience with clear maps of what is where, and where we will be going, the guests will soon feel at home. This will mean they will soon begin to relax and enjoy this time away from the office. It's a treat.

Thinking of some of the activities you might do on holiday, I am sure you will understand what happens next. This is a package deal. The guests do not just turn up and go their own way. Some will need an introduction to new concepts: this is how you windsurf, this is how you dive safely, this is how you snorkel, this is how you abseil. A good instructor will help the new 'recruits' get to know their equipment and new skills in the minimum possible time. This is *new* knowledge.

Thinking of some of the activities you might do on holiday will help to understand the difference between 'Entrance' – learning the procedures – and 'Switching OwNership' – going it alone; choosing our own activities and building our own memories.

All of the above can be outlined in the brochure, yet what happens next is the most significant part of a perfect holiday. As holiday-makers, your experience switches from a resort-directed experience to your own choices. Having grasped the basic skills and safety procedures, you are ready to go solo.

At the 'Switching OwNership' phase of the holiday and model, YOU have the joy of making it YOUR holiday!

You choose the activities you want to spend your time on. In an instant the experience moves out of the brochure and into your own personal memories. This is the phase of the model that we call 'Switching OwNership' – where learners both 'Switch On' to the possibilities and 'Switch Ownership' in that they are 'owning' the process and making their own choices. In the training model, this is where the trainer becomes the facilitator and helps learners apply their own unique blends of intelligences to the learning they have been exposed to. This allows the learners to personalize or 'own' the learning.

Experiencing a holiday 'to the full' often includes making a record to 'Store' those unique memories for later recall.

The next phase of the model is 'Store'. On your holiday you will have all manner of ways to store your experiences for later recall. Firstly, there is the positive emotional experience that goes straight into long-term memory. Secondly, you are likely to send postcards back to your friends describing your experience. What a brilliant idea for a training workshop: getting our 'holiday-makers' to send a postcard to themselves or their colleagues describing their learning experiences – 'Wish you were here'. Furthermore, we have all the technical aids: cameras and video recorders. Some people even phone home, with so many delegates insisting on picking up their mobile phones during the breaks in learning, we could proactively ask them to phone someone to tell them what they are learning.

During the 'Store' phase, we want to be able to store for later communication a key summary of our experience – like a postcard from holiday.

Curt Lewin has suggested that telling someone about your experiences can improve your chances of *acting* on your experience tenfold. In the training model we may even use digital photos to help remember the contributions the group made to make the learning a unique experience. Tony Buzan's Mind Mapping is a wonderful memory 'postcard' too. Above all, it is important to tell someone else the key summary of what you have experienced so that you benefit from the truism: 'expression deepens impression', or put another way, 'what you pay attention to e-x-p-a-n-d-s'.

The next phase in your perfect holiday experience is called 'Act'. This is where you demonstrate to yourself what you have experienced. In the holiday metaphor it may be similar to 'Store' in you telling someone else about your adventures or showing off your new skill or tan! However, the emphasis is on 'giving out' at this stage – whereas 'Store' is about 'taking in' with a view to making a keep-sake.

'Act' is about showing your learning or experience to others – perhaps by having a slide show?

You may have a few friends round to show them your holiday snaps or videos. This flows naturally into the 'Go-Again' phase where you literally 'Go-Again' over your experiences, reviewing them (often literally re-viewing). This sends a clear message to your nervous system that this experience was significant and that it should become a strong reference point for judging the quality of other experiences. This may also mean that you are 'still on holiday' when you get back to work. Well, surely this is what we want from a training intervention? We want the new techniques, attitudes, skills and knowledge to be foremost in the learners' minds when they go back to work. In this way we can guarantee greater value from the investment in training because there will be a higher degree of skill transfer. Often when colleagues come back from a great holiday, they bring a little bit of that holiday with them. They may be bronzed on the outside and also sunny within, radiating that inner calm that true recreation stirs up within us.

The review phase of the model/holiday is called 'Go-Again' when we reflect upon our holiday/learning experience in a deeply relaxed state.

In the training model, 'Act' is usually a 'game show' style activity to help learners realize how smart they are with their new discoveries. 'Go-Again' then becomes a wonderful review experience where learners relax deeply (like being in a hammock on a tropical hideaway location) while the holiday tour guide takes them once again through the joys they have experienced. If this does not sound like the normal kind of training workshop you attend, then may I invite you to experience one? I have found it to be transformational.

'What shall I do next year?' This is the essence of the 'Engage' phase.

The final phase of our model, and of the perfect holiday cycle, is called 'Engage'. This is where we build 'memories of the future' and make decisions – 'Was that good for me? Do I want to go there again, or shall I plan to go somewhere else in future?' A fantastic training experience helps the learners visualize clearly the 'where next?' and 'what next?'

We build for tomorrow by celebrating the magic of today. This is far more than 'action planning'. It is more a case of building deliberate future scenarios; how can we utilize our experiences of the holiday/learning and where can we see ourselves going with them next in order to enrich our experiences one step further? It 'engages' our motivation, our commitment and our desire, and keeps the vision in-sight, in-mind. It is a promise to the future.

This, in essence, is Accelerated Learning. The result is that we learn faster in a more pleasant way. This allows the learning to last longer as an enduring, pleasant and practical memory. Furthermore, the learning discoveries go deeper, becoming a part of us that we wish to grow and develop. This is the joy of learning.

Figure 1 is an overview Mind Map of the whole model. Have a quick look at it now, and then please take at least a 4 minute break before moving on to the next section.

Summary

Accelerated Learning and Training works so powerfully because it taps into the same motivations that make learning a hobby or going on holiday such a pleasure. It has all the elements of an excellent holiday: great expectations beforehand, the buzz of the arrival at the holiday destination, the thrill of discovery, the liberty of doing your own thing, the feel-good factor of collecting mementos, the joy of sharing your experiences with others, the pleasure of reviewing what a great time you had, and dreaming about future opportunities. Since the M.E.S.S.A.G.E.™ design framework is based on what we naturally enjoy, it is naturally successful.

PHASE ONE

Mindset and Mindsetting – *Make Ready!*

Learners come with their own ready made set of expectations.

Our journey towards designing and delivering excellent Accelerated Training begins well before the event. Learners do not just appear out of nowhere, nor do they wake up one morning and think that this day is the day they will attend an Accelerated Learning workshop. Furthermore, learners do not come empty to an event – they bring their experiences, both helpful and not so, their prejudices, their psychological baggage and other distractors, as well as their expectations. All these are mapped out in their own unique colour chart of the universe by which they navigate their own version of reality.

Key benefit: a faster, longer, deeper kind of magic.

I am sure that you have experienced certain workshops where the magic is just right. The right group, the right time, the right place, the right facilitator, the right subject, the right group-think. By choosing responsibility for taking action before the event, the Accelerated Trainer can help this magic happen by design, rather than by chance. Remember successful Accelerated Learning is like a faster, longer, deeper kind of magic. We learn faster, keep the results longer, and integrate at a deeper level – leading to more transfer and transformation of learning into habitual behaviours and use of knowledge. When compared with more conventional approaches, this appears quite magical in its efficacy.

Trainer communicates in advance with course participants with a view to setting realistically expanded expectations.

Advanced communication

I have deliberately chosen to use ambiguous grammar here – 'advanced' rather than 'advance' because Accelerated Training design and delivery uses both communication in advance of an event, and communication that is advanced linguistically.

Most trainers have a need to send out some sort of joining instructions. Whilst much of this is done via e-mail today, I still prefer the reassuring thud of a hefty packet landing when the post is delivered. Most learners still love the post when it brings good news, and an Accelerated Learning event is good news.

Whichever medium we choose to open communications, let us get enthusiastic about the learning beginning at this point. With brilliant planning and design, we can have our team of learners ready to go and open-minded before they even arrive.

Let us also use the other energy levels available to us. A phone call has more personal energy and higher interactive dynamism than any form of mail. Finally, a face-to-face meeting offers people the greatest amount of opportunity to understand the subtleties of communication.

A PREVIEW SCHEDULE

A Preview Schedule of contact maximizes learner readiness, and minimizes attrition.

To maximize the impact of an event that is planned well in advance, we can mirror the review schedule that we encounter during the 'Engage' phase of our model, creating a preview schedule.

We can benefit from seeding expectations, attention and interest as much as three months in advance of the event. I know from my own

Perseverance pays! You may need to 'influence' someone nine times before they commit.

Pre-course reading can work well.

A Welcome Pack that uses a range of media means that we will keep most of the people happy most of the time.

experience of sales and marketing that many of my customers begin their journey towards training with my organization as much as nine months in advance. I also know that many people need seven to nine exposures to a buying proposition before they finally buy-in. This can be a cause of encouragement for us: perseverence pays.

What I am talking about here is working with people three months in advance of the event, *after* they have bought in. There will be some general ideas you can help them discover this far in advance, especially any background reading. For example, at Buzan Centres we have found it useful to ask prospective new Buzan trainers to read certain books by Tony Buzan this far in advance and then to send us their Mind Maps® of their understanding. In this way, the transfer of learning and ownership begins well in advance.

THE WELCOME APPROACH

The next key milestone on the journey is one month in advance. The welcome approach can come at several energy levels. E-mail has the power of immediacy as it is accelerated both in delivery and potential response time. It is also flexible, the learner being able to open it when convenient. The same degree of flexibility is also offered by paper-based post, with the added advantage of knowing that the contents can be opened, which is not always the case with e-mail attachments! I like post as part of the welcome approach because it is then so easy to use a variety of media in one package – coloured Mind Maps®, an audio recording (tape or CD), even video or DVD, marketing and informative documentation, questionnaires to fill in and fax back, in short, an engaging and exciting activity pack.

This is where the full welcome pack works well, complete with joining instructions, testimonials, pre-course work, contact numbers, FAQs, a preview poster, recorded previews; your imagination and your budget are the only limits.

Attention

Interest

Desire

Action

Utilizing marketing insights, we are seeking to build expectations through four key stages: attention, interest, desire and action. This simple formula has proven marketing success, and, like it or not, learning is as much about marketing your knowledge proposition as it is about the content itself.

This is where it pays to watch adverts and read junk mail. What works well? What turns you off? When it comes to delivering congruently, you must be switched-on before you have any chance of switching-on other people to the learning; therefore, any advertizing that works for you will be congruent with the approach you can take, matching your own style.

A week in advance it pays to up the energy level and make that telephone call. This gives you long enough to make any necessary adjustments to logistics or to address any learner doubts of their own ability or course relevance.

Finally, time a card mailing for the day or so before just to build the expectation that something really special is going to happen. With any programme that invites a shift in personal paradigms, postcards with visual illusions work well. A simple salutation and a challenge are all you will need:

'Out of sight . . .'

> 'Hi, A N Other,
> The event on (whenever) is a chance to have another great day so I thought you might like to begin thinking about our time together now. Here's something to stimulate your interest and curiosity – what do YOU see?'

If it's not joyous, it's not Accelerated Learning.

My rationale for this approach comes from a common English cliché. Perhaps you could finish it for me? 'Out of sight . . .' If 'out of sight' really does lead to 'out of mind', then there will be a very simple way to gain in-sights. To gain insights, the ideas must be in-mind. By being there in the participants' minds, in a way that adds to the quality of their life (rather than being a nuisance), you help the learners prepare themselves for a life-enriching experience. The concept that I have most enjoyed learning from Georgi Lozanov's approach is that the hallmark of Accelerated Learning is joy. If it is not joyous, it is not Accelerated Learning.

A WORD ABOUT WAVELENGTHS

'Wavelengths' are an important concept for our approach. I use the concept both metaphorically and literally when it comes to brain-waves.

We only pay attention to those things we have programmed into our minds as being significant.

We are all tuning in to the world around us, even when we are asleep. We filter our experience to see if it matches our expectations and experience of reality. When there is an approximate match, our system wakes up the conscious mind's awareness of the event, and draws its attention to the sensory stimulus. When sensory events happen that are outside our programmed field of experience or interest, our other-than-conscious mind does not disturb the work the conscious mind is currently paying attention to. In relationships, this can be both amusing and irritating. Thus, we can learn to tune-out to our loved ones when we are engrossed in other activities, not even looking up when they say a friendly greeting. Or, we can be in a busy airport and catch the unique sound signature of our loved one's voice amidst the clamouring crowds, enabling us to find them and celebrate our reunion.

We tune-in to the sights, sounds and feelings that are meaningful.

There are many facts of life that we will examine as we journey along together – facts that we cannot change and therefore need to work with. Tuning-out and tuning-in are two such facts that the Accelerated Trainer must learn to work with.

One wavelength that everyone tunes in to is WIIFM? ('What's In It For Me?', not 'We're In It For Money' as a participant recently volunteered on a programme!) In order to give our commitment to anything, we must know what is in it for us – what the benefit will be. It is therefore important throughout the Mindset phase that we broadcast benefits.

The features of what we offer need to be transformed into benefits before we can expect our target learners to share our excitement.

Many communicators get excited about the features of their approach – after all it is *their* approach. They may have qualifications and experiences that they have worked hard for. However, this may not impress the prospective learners unless it can be translated into a benefit that matches the wavelength they are tuned in to.

An easy way to take your experience and transform it into a signal that others can relate to is to ask two simple questions.

1. Which means that . . .?
2. So what?

'Sell the sizzle, not the sausage . . .'

It is all about selling the benefit of what a thing can do for us, not what it actually is. Let us use an example to illustrate. Accelerated Learning encourages the dominance of two brain-wave states: alpha waves, for learning new information, and theta waves, for deep integration of learned material. These are two features of our approach.

If we ask ourselves, 'Which means that . . .?' we begin to think in terms of what the alpha and theta waves do for us. Alpha waves help us learn new material at a faster rate. Theta waves help us integrate material at the deeper levels of consciousness.

In key industries like the Health Service, getting people back to work as soon as practical is a key benefit.

These are 'advantages'. These themselves may be enough for our partner in communication to say, 'Got it – now I understand and am interested.' However, it is still useful to ask the second question, 'So what?' If we learn at a faster rate, we have more time available to learn more or to use to deal with other demands on our time. Some of my work is with the National Health Service. To take nurses, doctors, managers and consultants away from their frontline roles means that patients are getting less attention. It is therefore a key benefit of Accelerated Learning that my clients can get their skills updated and upgraded in the shortest period of time. *This* is the wavelength my Health Service customers are tuned-in to.

If theta waves help us integrate levels of material at a deeper level, we can then have these materials as a well-established resource to draw upon. What normally happens is that delegates enjoy a learning experience and then are thrown back in at the deep end of demands on their attention. There is little time to integrate the learning so that it becomes natural or 'second-nature'. It is only when learning becomes 'second- nature' that we are likely to find ourselves using it habitually.

By activating a theta-dominant state where deep integration happens, we can ensure the highest likelihood that the learners will actually *apply* their new learning back in the intended theatre of experience.

ction

Figure 2 gives you a simple chart to work through to translate the features you are offering into the language of benefits, with an example given to help you.

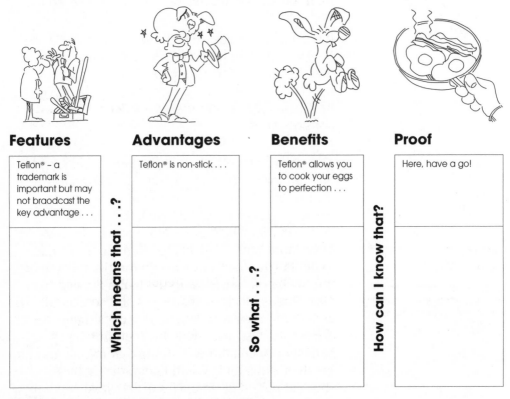

Figure 2   Transforming features into benefits

The first and last four minutes of any communication event are defining moments of truth. They set the scene for what happens next . . .

this phase of our model is all about *make ready!*
Our goal is to bring our learners to a state of readiness, willingness and, finally, ability.

The welcoming environment

THE FIRST FOUR MINUTES

It has been suggested that in western culture we only have four minutes to make a lasting impression. This means that the first four minutes of any Accelerated Learning event are important to set the scene for success. I do not remember the last programme I ran when everyone was there on time – not even on the residential courses! Every late arrival resets the clock for the four minute lasting impression. This 'stop-start', 'stop-start' does not allow a smooth transition into the flow of a training day.

What can we do? I have begun to launch programmes bang on time with something that stimulates those who have made it on time. However, I defer those activities that we shall be discussing later that allow delegates to lay aside distractions, clear their minds for learning and focus on the specific objectives. The reason is simple; those who are late are often the ones who need most help in clearing the clutter before they learn.

Starting programmes on time, whether all delegates are there or not is important, but leaving the 'clearing activity' until everyone is there is vital. Therefore, I hold this valuable activity about 30 minutes into a workshop.

YOU ARE THE KEY

You are the key.

An important concept throughout this work will be *'entrainment'*. This is a 'frequency-following response' – a response by our nervous system to a sensory stimulus. When the senses hook on to an image, a sound, a change in environment, or especially a smell, we then respond by transforming our mindset into the one that most appropriately matches the last time we experienced such a stimulus.

Love at first sight.

This is how you get 'love at first sight'. There will be a visual, auditory, physical or olfactory stimulus that matches your bio-database's records for arousal and imprinting. Before you can stop it, your chemistry experiment boils over, and you are smitten.

The very nature of an Accelerated Training event guarantees that there will be myriad stimuli to set off delegates' associations. This is usually good, but we can also be prepared for adverse entrainment. Someone who associates non-hierarchical seating and strong visuals with a juvenile approach to education may respond by regarding the learning as facile or not serious enough.

Whatever your delegates' initial first four minute response to your creative learning environment, one thing is certain: your presence is the key. You can make or destroy the atmosphere within those four minutes.

Many trainers, when they sense hostility, move into a defensive or apologetic mode. This can be disastrous. If you believe in your approach, it does not need defending. In theory your delegates have been prepared for the culture shock through the advanced communication. If they are still not happy, it is they who need to shift their openness. You will be confident that all the principles in this publication are naturally brain-friendly; which is why they work. Your mission thus becomes to help the resistant delegates remove their own self-imposed associative barriers to new learning experiences.

One key way to do this is to stay positive and to spout benefits whilst 'mind-reading' what the delegates may be thinking. 'You may be asking yourself, "Why are there coloured pens all over the tables?" We have decided to offer colour as an option today because of its positive impact on memory recall. In fact, Tony Buzan in *Use Your Memory* states that it can improve memory recall by as much as 50 per cent.' With the right positive frame, any proposition can be accepted.

Your body language often has more impact.

Use your body! Your body language often has more impact at the other-than-conscious level than your words. Language can also be your ally. Using multi-sensory language to describe your benefits, outcomes and content will help the group literally 'make sense' of where you are coming from.

I sometimes practice writing descriptions of a training event using as many sensory words as I can think of. It is very satisfying. You can also model that it is acceptable to play and to make mistakes.

Personal contact is enhanced through your natural smile, your use of appropriate names, healthy eye-contact, and appropriate humour. I am not a fan of political correctness. I recognize its positive intention and its appropriateness, but also suggest that it is not a reflection of natural communication. Much of the spark in life comes from humour and taking risks. Only you will be able to judge each unique group and situation.

Enthusiasm is contagious – and often irritating. This is another driver to watch. Yes, of course you should be enthusiastic. However, one of our key skills will be to notice where the energy level of the group is and come in with our energy level just slightly above theirs. This will then help us lift them higher at a sensible rate of ascent. Above all, behavioural flexibility is our best friend. Without rapport we are a non-starter and any trainer knows that what works with one group can be really off-putting for another group. Develop acuity and adaptability.

Broadcast your expectation that each learner will succeed.

Finally, broadcast verbally and non-verbally your own expectations of success. No doubt you will have experienced the effect where someone else's expectations strongly influence your performance? We tend to get more of what we expect. This is simply because our senses selectively filter our experience and present information that matches our expectations of reality to our conscious mind. If you radiate positive expectations of the group enjoying and succeeding in their learning adventure, it will encourage their senses to scan for evidence that backs up your assertion.

Using 'Yes tags' can help you help learners get themselves into a positive frame of mind.

How many times have you heard trainers say, 'Now this next bit is probably the hardest section we'll be looking at . . .' Again, I understand the positive intention, but this is disastrous psychology. Use a different frame. For example, 'This next section is easy if you break it into small enough parts . . . which I've been doing for the last three years – so let's see for ourselves how easy we can make it, shall we?' The 'shall we?' is what Peter Thomson calls a 'Yes tag'; a linguistic marker that encourages us to answer 'Yes!' If we can encourage 'Yes' responses in our delegates' minds, they will soon feel more confident about their own abilities to learn.

MULTIPLE IDENTITIES

Our outcome is to promote a continuing state of relaxed awareness. Key messages are that learning will be safe and confidential, and that experimentation is welcome. Lozanov even allows his delegates to adopt a new identity for the training so that mistakes can be made in the name of the adopted character. This allows delegates to take risks and be more adventurous. I remember one presentation skills programme where the delegates became phobic when the video camera was brought out! I suggested they become their favourite presenter and had a go *as* their heroine or hero. The transformation was 'miraculous'. It is just another idea that works!

ROOM LAYOUT

Many positive 'subliminal' messages can be broadcast by arranging your work area to allow for space for activities, non-hierarchical seating, adequate ventilation, variable temperature controls, natural light sources, positive well-positioned peripherals and work areas ready for learners' involvement. Perhaps the most useful thing I have found is to be explicitly permissive about letting the learners change the environment to suit themselves.

PERIPHERAL STIMULI

We can influence the other-than-conscious mind through the strategic use of peripheral stimuli such as posters, props, music and anything that pleases the senses.

Most of the materials I have researched on Accelerated Learning were not new to me, I was doing some 'Accelerated Learning' without realizing the 'how' and the 'why'. However, there were areas that were new to me, one of which was the impact of peripheral stimuli on the other-than-conscious mind. Our conscious mind is easily engaged and distracted but our wiser and more experienced other-than-conscious mind tracks all the other events that are happening in our environment. This allows us to suggest all manner of positive messages through posters, props and sensory enrichment. Many of the venues I use are 'sterile' and 'institutionalized' with a stale smell. I have found that lemon or lime spray adds a freshness that delegates respond positively to first thing in the morning. Aromatherapy is very fascinating; however, you should be aware of some of the perceived risks of the use of some essential oils during pregnancy. Many pregnant delegates are nervous about the use of essential oils. Pure citrus sprays preclude this problem arising.

There are now so many ways to prepare and present content-relevant artwork that your imagination is the limit. I use positive personal affirmations, motivational quotes, affirmations that learning is easy, enjoyable, effective and important, and subject-specific messages. One surprise was to find that we tune-out to peripherals after about three weeks. So, organizations that have invested a fortune on motivational posters will get more value for their money if they move the posters around every three weeks.

Correct *spelling* is critical.

One important poster that Colin Rose recommends is the welcome poster. This can easily be personalized and can often lend itself to a topical theme. Spelling is critical! The tone also may be very important; not everyone wants to start on first name terms. With a little bit of imagination, you can also incorporate Buzan, brain-friendly concepts such as dimension and multiple colours to really make the impact something special. This, of course, is also fun for you! Make your poster a key focal point.

SONIC ENTRAINMENT

Entrainment is the physical and biological phenomenon where systems synchronize with each other. For example, a baby that rests for long enough against its mother's breast will change its heartbeat to be in synchrony with its mother's heartbeat.

Music with a strong beat can assist the learning experience.

Music is a very important and powerful 'beat signature' to encourage the mind to get into synch with the learning experience. It is one of the most exciting and dangerous areas of Accelerated Learning. Firstly, it is usually used illegally! Readers in the UK can contact the Performing Right Society at Elwes House, 19 Church Walk, Peterborough, PE1 2UZ. The PRS issue licences to venues so that they can legitimately use pre-recorded works to enhance the working environment.

Secondly, it is a major entrainer. Most of us have very clear associations and associative emotional states linked to key musical pieces. If you use well-known popular artists, you can potentially provoke more of a distraction than a learning enhancement. For this reason, I tend to use less well-known pieces but in a clearly recognizable style. I am very careful with volume, keeping it low for most purposes. I also recommend a wide selection of tracks for each purpose so that there are several fall-back positions.

To avoid any danger of existing associations with current music, a solution is to compose music specifically for the learning process. As a composer, one of the areas I am really enjoying exploring is composing music to match a certain beat, harmonic framework and emotional mood specifically for accessing and encouraging various mindsets. You can follow the progress of these projects on our website: *www.lexstudios.com*

The fastest way to begin harnessing the power of music is to take some time aside now to generate a list of at least five tracks under each of the following headings:

- ○ Music for entrances
- ○ Music for exits
- ○ Music for transitions
- ○ Music for group energizing
- ○ Music for relaxation and review
- ○ Music to change mindset during breaks
- ○ Music to facilitate rhythmic learning
- ○ Music to empower imagery and visualization
- ○ Music to emphasize specific learning points from your key programmes.

To make this easy for yourself, think of the emotional states associated with each of the headings, perhaps listing them first. Then match tracks to those emotional states that will work for you. For example, a whole genre of music for relaxation, review and chill out was created in the 1980s, beginning with the Café del Mar. The whole purpose of this music was to create a mood of relaxation after a hard night's clubbing. This would seem very suitable for anyone who needs to relax after a difficult journey to the training venue.

The other main sonic entrainment device is your voice. Popular movies often display the impact of an accent or tone or speed of voice upon the characters. Experiment! Get a voice coach. Your voice is one of the most important tools you have, so it is worth investing in.

Your voice is one of the most important tools you have.

LEARNING PROPS

Physical representations of learning points, for example models, are very powerful ways to anchor the learning experience so that it can be easily recalled. I also use readily available games, such as Buckaroo, as a way of illustrating and experiencing key messages.

Connecting and clearing

If we are to help learners get more of what they want in life, we need to be able to relate to where they are now and their present state of mind. A simple way to begin this connecting process is to find out their names, roles and what was on their minds as they came to the seminar. This is such an easy way to establish 'Where are we now?', giving us our first bearing as we set course for 'Where do we intend to get to?' You can also facilitate the process by being the first to share this information and letting the group know your state of mind.

CLEARING THE MIND FOR LEARNING

The following process has been so successful over the years that it now appears in all my workshops that are longer than an hour. It has also leaked into the way I manage meetings and my own personal mental management when I need to focus. I believe that you will find it as invaluable as it is simple to apply.

The process revolves around the natural organizing principles of our working memory. In short, we can only multi-task five to nine concepts, or seven plus-or-minus two (7 ± 2) before our 'system' crashes. A crash can be as simple as your mind going blank, or as complex as becoming emotionally confused and anxious without knowing the cause.

Focused Mind	
Your Attractors	Your Distractors
Define your outcome	Park your good ideas and other 'things to do'. Store any emotional distractors in a safe place for dealing with later. Dump any distracting mental 'rubbish'.

Figure 3   Connecting and clearing

Figure 3 is a copy of a handout I give to my delegates when we go through the process of closing down distractors. If the working memory can only cope with seven plus-or-minus two units of attention, then it follows that we can do our mental processing a service by *shutting down* the 'programmes' we do not need. We often run 'programmes' in working memory that would be better shunted off to a paper-based memory for reloading or deleting later.

For example, have you ever had another driver 'borrow' your lane and found yourself reacting, either internally or even out loud? Well, if you are anything like me, something like that can affect the rest of my journey, if not my day, and this is the sort of 'garbage' that I can afford to trash. However, many of us will carry our 'road rage' (and other forms of rage against 'injustice') around with us as our companion throughout the working day. Therefore distractors such as these are better closed down and 'thrown into the bin' – they should be written in the right-hand column.

Trash the garbage . . .

Lock away emotional distractors
until later . . .

Emotive programmes take up more processing power than other programmes, so they can consume our attention and interfere with other thinking. For example have you ever been misunderstood? Out of the goodness of your heart, you share something precious with someone else who promptly fails to ascribe to it the same value as you put upon it. Naturally, you are offended! This is material that now has an emotional charge and we have already discussed the fact that the emotional centre of the brain and the long-term memory are one and the same system. Unlike the garbage, emotive programmes don't bin very well. Emotional baggage needs to be dealt with *at an appropriate time*. So, emotionally charged material also goes in the right-hand column in the metaphorical 'safe'. Here it can be locked away so that it doesn't leak into the rest of our thinking and we can unlock it later so that it can be handled safely. If we don't do the equivalent of this exercise, emotions have a way of leaking into the rest of our thinking for the day. I am sure you have been in meetings that have been compromised by hidden agendas that have nothing to do with the objectives of the meeting. State of mind and mindset is everything.

Not all distractors are 'bad', so
park any other business . . .

The document is there throughout the whole workshop in case anything else crops up because distractors are not all bad. Many are important ideas, issues or things to do which would otherwise weigh on our minds. However, these too can interfere with our concentration, so we 'park' them in our distractor column with the emotional baggage and needless garbage. Why don't we just forget the garbage? The answer is simply because we *don't* forget the garbage. If we write it down, we can draw our conscious mind's attention to the fact that we have paid the concept its fair dues of attention and that it is now on one side as dealt with.

The left-hand column is the flip side of this exercise. It is very good to clear our minds for learning, yet the mind abhors a vacuum. It is one thing to close down programmes to free up processing power, quite another to *load* the programme focus of our choice. This is why the exercise has a WIIFM section so that we can tune our senses to seek out those attractors,the objects of desire, in other words, more of what we really want.

ON ROLES AND RULES

One of the most useful concepts I have adopted from transactional analysis is that of 'contracting' with my clients. This often takes the form of the 'roles and rules' that map out our mutual expectations and in workshops I have found it useful to make these explicit.

As trainers, we believe it is the host organization's responsibility to provide resources and support to help the learning come on-line back in the workplace but it is also the individual learner's responsibility to 'own' their learning, to bring their experience to the learning, to commit to contributing, to take part in the group process and to review the lessons that they can take away with them. One of our outcomes is to encourage self-directed learning.

Sometimes I have found it necessary to include some principles in workshops such as: asking questions via the trainer, keeping to agreed timings and making mistakes as an expected approach to mastery of new skills. I also believe it is the participants' right to not participate, provided it is for positive learning reasons.

Other roles and rules include the client organization's right to receive feedback from the delegates on how valuable they found the training.

Therefore, most of us have to endure the chore of 'happy sheets' at the end of workshops. However, I am sure I speak for many of us when I suggest that these are missing the point. Yes, it is important that the trainer does a professional and effective job of communicating new information, but it is not the most important point. What is far more important is that the learner has a chance to articulate how specifically they will take ownership and commit to putting the learning into action. I live for the day when we trainers turn the tables and evaluate the organizations and clients we work with; they are the stars of the show and they are the ones who need the feedback and support more than we do. The Chartered Institute of Personnel and Development (CIPD) in the UK are to be applauded for the feedback they ask their consultants to give on the consultant's evaluation of the client organization and the delegates. May this practice spread.

As a trainer, I also believe it is our responsibility to provide a clear structure, excellent materials, appropriate activities and theories. It is our responsibility to answer questions and address issues honestly, even if that answer is, 'I don't know.' It is also our mission to facilitate success. Finally, we do need to be aware of and responsible for aspects of health and safety.

WELL-FORMED THINKING

Beware of Woolly Thinkers!

Many people will not think if they can get away with it! When clarifying outcomes as a trainer, with a view to delivering what the delegates really want, you will often encounter woolly thinking. This will not serve the learners if they are really to move towards a clearly desired state.

Here is a P.O.W.E.R.F.U.L. way of achieving clarity. Well-formed outcomes adhere to the following guidelines. P.O.W.E.R.F.U.L. is a mnemonic to remind us of the key principles: positive; owned; WIIFM; evidenced; resourced; faith-filled; unique; living.

As a coach you would have the time to take a client through each of these criteria step by step. A different approach is necessary as a trainer. I recommend that you memorize and apply the eight criteria to your own goals. Once you become familiar with them, you will 'hear' a breach of one

Frame goals towards what you would rather have . . .

rather than away from what you want to avoid . . .

and make sure the outcome is something you can influence . . .

then find a 'win' that is really compelling.

of these key principles when a delegate expresses a woolly goal. Often it is enough just to ask a key question to get them back on target. I have included an example question for each criterion.

Positive: An outcome that is framed in positive terms helps us get our attention on what we want. We know that what we pay attention to e-x-p-a-n-d-s in our awareness. If our goal is to quit smoking, our focus will be on . . . smoking! If you find your delegates are articulating negative outcomes – something they do not want as a result of your programme – ask them a simple question: 'What would you rather have?' I am currently overweight. If I concentrate on losing weight, my whole attention is on how fat I feel. If I shift my attention to how slim I would like to be, my energy and attention shifts to the positive.

Owned: If we are to influence our progress, it makes sense to set goals that we can control the outcomes of. If I say I want more people to like my training, I have yielded the control over to whomever the 'people' are. If I own the goal, I will frame it in terms such as, 'I want to make my training more enjoyable.' A good question to ask here would be 'How can you take responsibility for this?'

WIIFM: We sometimes fail to follow-through in pursuing our goals because there is not a big enough benefit to make them compelling. If you are falling short of something you want to achieve – attach a bigger 'win' to the pursuit of your goal by constantly asking yourself, 'What will this do for me?' until you eventually get to a 'win' that is compelling enough to fuel your efforts to achieve your aspiration.

For example if I want to be able to read music but have never got around to it, I may ask myself the question and get the answer of: 'It's useful in my job'. However, this may still not be enough of a 'win' for me to make time, so if I ask again, and get: 'I will be able to play more tunes on my piano', this may be a more compelling 'win' for me.

What will I see, hear and feel that will give me the evidence that I am achieving my goal?

And what resources will I need?

Act 'as if' you are already living your dream: 'What would it feel like if this were already true?'

Keep your goals distinct, separating them when they overlap.

Evidenced: We can mentally set ourselves to notice our progress towards achieving more of what we would like in life if we let our imaginations run a programme of what fulfilling our dreams will look, sound, feel, taste and smell like. Since we get more of what we pay attention to, this will help our senses scan for the right cues. A question for delegates here could be: 'What will you see, hear and feel that will let you know that you are achieving this goal?'

Resourced: Many brilliant ventures fail through poor marketing, support or other resourcing. It really pays to consider: 'What resources will I need to achieve this goal?' These resources can then be part of incremental goals if necessary.

Faith-filled: If you get into the habit of reading self-development literature you will eventually come across a fascinating paradox. When we wish for something, we rarely get it. This is because wishing is to do with the future. Future goals do not have to be fulfilled until tomorrow, which never comes. In St Mark's Gospel, Jesus tells his disciples (learners) that whatever they ask for in prayer will be done for them *if* they believe they *have* received it (Mark 11:24). This is similar to much later psychological injunctions to act *as if* something was true. In terms of what we have been discovering about how our nervous system works, we can see the sense in this. If we hold a clear vision of what it is we wish to see in our lives *as if* it is already here, our senses will filter our experience to notice anything that suggests our vision is coming true. Therefore, the question could be: 'What would it feel like if this were already true?'

Unique: We can confuse the nervous system if we seek to load overlapping programmes. Health and fitness are excellent goals, but they are not the same. We can be healthy yet not fit and vice versa. Help your delegates to keep their goals unique, simple and discrete. 'Are you certain this is a distinct goal, or is it really several?' Health is one goal; fitness is a separate goal.

One powerful way to achieve our goals . . .

is to refocus upon them early in the day.

Living: Most of us have experienced the frustration of a computer crash. The mind is like a computer in that it sometimes 'crashes'. For example, the times when you just cannot think straight and you need to do the equivalent of a computer rebooting its system, by taking a break or having a good night's sleep. However, once you have 'rebooted', you need to reload the 'programme' which was the focus of your thinking. One very powerful way to achieve our goals is to refocus upon them early in the day.

Brian Tracey, the Canadian motivational speaker taught me a very easy way to do this. 'How can you keep this goal in sight in mind every day?' Buy an attractive notebook, and each and every day, write in it your 'core life goals' and your specific focus for that day. This loads the programme and keeps your dreams, direction and vision as a living reality.

Summary

I trust I have conveyed that until the Mindset is appropriate for Accelerated Learning, there is no point in proceeding. Furthermore, if someone's state of mind shifts away from an optimum state for learning during *any part* of the M.E.S.S.A.G.E.™ model it is imperative that we return to address the needs of the right Mindset. Only then can we re-engage the process.

Many things influence our Mindset. Some are subtle such as the peripheral stimuli of music, art, temperature and lighting. Others are more direct such as the attitude of the trainer and the specific attention to laying aside all distractions, clearing the mind for learning. Mindsetting begins in advance through the wise use of expectation setting and of advanced communication.

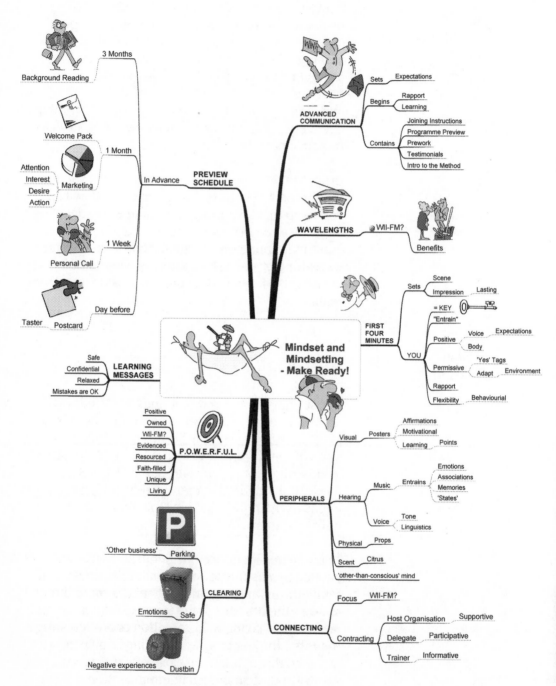

Figure 4 A review Mind Map of the Mindset phase

Entrance is about new ideas gaining entrance to our conscious learning process. The method we use is literally to *make sense!* By designing and delivering fresh content that stimulates our three dominant senses of seeing, hearing and feeling, we can keep most of our learners tuned-in most of the time.

The more ways we broadcast, the more people we tune in to.

PHASE TWO

Entrance – *Make Sense!*

Adult learning is a very different process to junior learning. By the time we are in our teens (and usually by the time we are seven) a fearsome but well-meaning gatekeeper has taken up residence in our minds.

Levels of consciousness

I call this sentient being 'the fanatic-in-the-attic'. This is because most of us can relate to the phenomenon of having a head full of mental chatter. Sometimes our brains are so busy that it seems difficult to get our thoughts to quieten down – they seem 'fanatical'.

It is very important to realize this is our logical mind acting as our internal critic. Its mission is to evaluate each new idea and opportunity and to decide whether they are in our interests or not. This is positive mental protection and often shields us from being taken advantage of. The downside is that any idea that is new to us is first regarded with suspicion in case it is 'dangerous'. The fact is we are most comfortable and secure with ideas that we are already familiar with; our comfort zone. If our minds are to be s-t-r-e-t-c-h-e-d to new dimensions – outside our comfort zone – there must be a suggestion that this will be worth the 'discomfort' of change.

The fanatic-in-the-attic must be convinced that it is safe to let go of previously accepted self-imposed barriers to new ideas and behaviours.

This is one of the reasons Lozanov talks about Suggestopaedia. Often, in order to free a mind to learn, we must first give it permission to let go of the suggestions that have made it difficult to learn, such as 'maths is hard' or 'no pain, no gain'; therefore learning must be difficult if it is true learning.

Our internal critic, 'the fanatic-in-the-attic', must be persuaded it is safe to let go of resistance to new ideas . . .

whereas the childlike mind learns by total immersion.

By way of contrast, the childlike unfettered mind learns by total immersion in the experience, playing, exploring and discovering without fear of mistakes.

In real terms the fanatic-in-the-attic can only really work on one thing at a time; this is our true conscious mind. However, like a computer that can run several programmes at once in the background, we too have background thoughts that float in and out of our direct attentions. This is the 7 ± 2 organizing principle of memory.

A common example is trying to concentrate in a meeting when out of nowhere your attention shifts to what you are going to be having for lunch. In that instant you lose the thread of the meeting.

Shifting attention can lose the thread of the meeting.

To make it easy to keep this distinction clear, let us talk about three levels of consciousness:

1. The **conscious mind** of the fanatic-in-the-attic can only concentrate on one thing at a time.
2. The **pre-conscious** mind can hold loosely 7 ± 2 areas of focus waiting to be actioned by the conscious mind. This is a funnel effect or filtering method.
3. Finally, below the threshold of conscious, is what Lozanov, Buzan and we call the **para-conscious** mind. The memory and

processing capacity of the para-conscious mind, to all intents and purposes is infinite. It holds the records of everything we've ever paid attention to and possibly everything in our peripheral awareness. You can imagine how overwhelming all this rich experience would be if it was suddenly presented to our conscious mind!

This is why we have the very elegant system of the infinite being filtered down to the 7 ± 2, which in turn is filtered down to the one highest priority at that particular moment.

When the pre-conscious mind is filled to capacity, this is when we feel we have a fanatic in our head. One of the most effective ways to Accelerate Learning is to clear all this mental clutter completely so that the full capacity of the pre-conscious mind is free to focus on up to 7 ± 2 aspects of our current priority.

In an ideal situation you will have cleared your mind for learning, focusing entirely upon the subject to be learned. The 7 ± 2 aspect of the pre-conscious would not be empty or idle but would be applied to interacting with the new ideas. For example, you would be comparing new concepts with your own experience, personalizing or even challenging the learning.

When we don't clear the pre-conscious mind effectively, we end up with a phenomenon of struggling to keep up with what an educator is presenting.

The para-conscious mind is below the floor of consciouness.

The para-conscious mind is our 'brain-in-the-basement' – as if it was below the floor of conscious. The pre-conscious mind is a function of the fanatic-in-the-attic.

Ultimately, Accelerated Training has to work with the co-operation of all three levels of mind. The gatekeeping fanatic-in-the-attic must be convinced the new ideas are safe and beneficial in order that the pre-conscious mind can be free to concentrate.

The whole state must be relaxed enough to allow insights from the para-conscious mind to percolate up from the 'basement' into conscious awareness.

CIRCUMNAVIGATING THE GATEKEEPING FANATIC

Of course, there are ways around the gatekeeper! Distract the fanatic-in-the-attic long enough and you can sneak ideas in. This is what advertizers, media gurus and politicians have been doing for decades. However, intention is everything. In Accelerated Training our intention is to enhance our capacity to learn through the co-operation of the fanatic!

The first way we choose to work with the fanatic-in-the-attic is to present a big picture.

The first way we work with the fanatic is to present the BIG picture.

The BIG picture

An important aspect of getting the conscious mind on board is enabling it to see a global overview of the journey ahead. This gives it a sense of context.

Since Accelerated Training is a new process to many learners it is valuable to give a BIG picture overview of not just the context but the actual process itself.

What then can we include in the process overview? Firstly, Accelerated Training benefits from group social learning. There is a poignant example of this in nature. Two British birds, the blue tit and the robin, have adapted their digestive systems to cope with milk; an unnaturally rich food source for them. In areas where milk is still delivered to the doorstep, blue tits and robins are common raiders of our milk supply, breaking through any foil top to steal the tasty drink beneath. Not *all* robins, however, are able to do this, whereas every blue tit has the capability. Is this because blue tits are smarter than robins? In

Social learning styles are more effective than solitary learning styles.

one sense, the answer is 'yes'. Blue tits are social birds whereas robins are territorial. Blue tits are group learners, sharing best practice; in this case, learning the best ways to break through a foil cap to the reward of the milk below. Robins are sole-learners, restricting best practice by keeping their 'trade secrets' to themselves.

So, a fundamental part of the Accelerated Training approach is a collaborative interdependent style of learning as modelled by blue tit social behaviour. Our groups *share* best practice. It means that investing time getting to know each other is perceived as a high-value activity for Accelerated Trainers.

This is a key advantage of group Accelerated Training over more solitary styles of learning such as computer-based training.

It also means that regular breaks are to be encouraged as an important part of the network learning process, rather than a necessary interruption of 'real' learning! Often, 'best practice' is more easily integrated and transferred over a lunch or refreshment break.

A second aspect to share in the BIG picture overview is the importance of clearing our minds for new learning as we have discussed in the Mindset phase.

Schedule a 'fluid level adjustment' every 45 minutes.

Thirdly, we can ensure the deliberate scheduling of brain breaks every 45 minutes. (Vanda North calls these 'fluid level adjustment' breaks!)

Fourthly, we can use multiple-intelligence and sensory enriched training techniques, such as using music, co-operative tasks, role rehearsal, imagery, stories, metaphors, games and activities.

One of the secrets of faster learning is to 'broadcast' our message using all the senses.

Fifthly, we can include a brief overview of the course content and, sixthly, we can flag the point that personal progress planning and reflection are also important parts of the schedule. This all acts as the equivalent of giving the learners the lid of the jigsaw before giving them the puzzle to construct, piece by piece.

THE MORE WAYS WE TEACH

We achieve a very high frequency of message transfer by sending out our signal on the visual (V) wavelength, the hearing (H) wavelength and the feeling (F) wavelength.

Colin Rose says, 'The more ways you teach, the more people you reach.' This is what we call b-r-o-a-d bandwidth broadcasting. VHF in radio means 'very high frequency'. In Accelerated Training it can have an additional meaning: visual, hearing, feeling. If we broadcast on VHF – visual, hearing and feeling – we will have a very high frequency of keeping most of the people happy most of the time. This is at the heart of our whole approach to the entrance of new material.

When we present fresh information to the three dominant senses, it literally 'makes sense'. When we don't include all three major senses, we are in danger of presenting 'non-sense'.

From dependence to independence to interdependence

Perhaps no one has popularized this continuum more than Stephen Covey. As it is important in life and relationships, so also it is important in learning. We want to start a revolution that allows learning to be recognized as something that happens everywhere, everywhen and everyhow.

The message needs to be clear: learning can happen within the group process without always requiring strong direction from the trainer. We can learn from each other.

If this message is accepted, the learners will naturally begin to recognize that every social interaction has learning potential, regardless of whether or not it is in the context of an official training event. Furthermore, every event in life is endowed with opportunities for fresh insights and learning.

One way to sow this message directly after the big picture overview is to set a team learning task that allows the group to discover its team learning potential. Examples of a team learning task might be the sharing of a pre-completed self-evaluation questionnaire of individual learning styles. The group could then divide themselves into clusters who share a strong learning preference; this could be a sensory preference such as visual, hearing or feeling but it all depends upon the type of questionnaire being used.

Groups can discover their team learning potential by being given a team learning task.

My favourite team activity involves the use of Neuland's 'pinpoint' boards. These are HUGE visual display boards on which the teams create a collage of their prior learning relevant to the topic in focus.

A subliminal message of independence can be sent to the group during this activity by the trainer physically leaving the room but you need to be confident that this will not have an adverse effect on the group. If you are at all unsure, you can 'busy yourself' with something so that you are 'apart' from the exercise but still somewhere in the room.

The content

Until Mindset is established, there is the ongoing danger of hidden agendas.

Up until now we have not even touched on the core content that we would like as a skills and knowledge transfer. This is because the frame sells the picture in Accelerated Training. Until Mindset is adequately catered for, there is no point in proceeding: there will only be the danger of hidden agendas or other mental distractions.

When we come to deliver the core content, we use many of the friends we have engaged along the journey so far. Foremost of these will be multi-sensory stimulation so that it 'makes sense'.

We will provide a BIG picture of the core content and of the learning objectives in a way that will encourage our delegates' senses. Then, when we deliver the content, we will deliberately design our presentation to stimulate the three dominant conscious senses: seeing, hearing and touch.

ENRICHING YOUR PRESENTATION VISUALLY

Take 10 minutes now to list some ways in which you feel you could make your visual aids more exciting.

Here are some ideas to accentuate your thinking. In neurolinguistic programming (NLP), the five senses are called sub-modalities. These are fine distinctions that make a tremendous difference.

To get your head around this, just consider how televisions are sold. The basic principle is the same, but there is a huge price difference when we introduce distinctions such as black and white versus colour, flat screen, LCD, sound enhancement and so on.

Key influencing factors visually are:
○ Size
○ Position
○ Clarity
○ Colour
○ Distinctiveness

Marketing research shows that we are influenced visually by size, position, clarity, colour and distinctiveness. These are examples of sub-modalities of the visual modality. Further examples can be found on the remote control, such as your personal preferences for colour, contrast and brightness. The implications of this are HUGE; changing the size of a learning visual aid can make the difference between a participant saying, 'I don't see it.' and, 'Now, I get the picture.'

In short, as a generalization, the larger and more colourful your visual aids, the more effective they tend to be. So, showing a training video on a 20 inch screen played on a VCR that isn't tracking properly could even have a detrimental effect. Playing a training DVD, using a computer projector onto a 6 foot screen will build far stronger learning associations.

Larger and more colourful tends to be more effective . . .

ENRICHING YOUR PRESENTATION SONICALLY

Take 10 minutes now to list some ways in which you feel you could make your presentation more sonically exciting.

Some of the sub-modalities of hearing can be found on a hi-fi remote, such as bass, treble, volume, balance, stereo and mono.

Key influencing factors sonically are:
○ Volume
○ Tone
○ Pace

As a generalization, the volume, tone and pace of your audio signal makes a BIG difference. For example if the sound is too loud, it will interfere more with the learning than if the sound is marginally too quiet.

The quality of your hi-fi equipment in the training room can enhance or detract. Even more important are the quality and variety of your vocal delivery. People can only know that you are enthusiastic if it is conveyed in your tone.

Presenting from a higher position, such as a lectern, says something about the authority of your message.

If possible, have more than one sound source. For example, some input from CD, input from the trainer and maybe a guest speaker. Experiment with where you present from within the training room. Participants can associate the tone of the communication with its location. Presenting from a lectern, for example, says something about the authority of your message, whilst sitting amongst the group gives a completely different message.

MAKING YOUR PRESENTATION MORE PHYSICAL

Take 10 minutes to list ways to get people more physically involved in the learning.

Key influencing factors physically are:
○ Movement
○ Location
○ Rhythm
○ Posture

Physical sub-modalities include movement, posture, temperature, texture, pressure, location and rhythm. So there is a VAST difference between presenting information on a flipchart compared with standing as a group and chanting the same information to a rhythm whilst stamping your feet!

Rhythmic learning fuses hearing and feeling and is very powerful when learning facts such as mathematical relationships. To try this for yourself, consider creating a physical continuum using the space available to you rather than a written chart. For example, you could stick a map on the wall and ask participants to place a colour dot where they come from or you could make it far more dramatic by turning the whole room into a spatial map.

When designing an Accelerated Training event, it makes sense to plan the delivery of fresh information using these three questions:

1. How can I enrich the visual component of my message?
2. How can I enrich my message sonically?
3. How can I get the participants more physically involved?

An ancient proverb says

'I hear, I forget;
I see, I remember;
I do, I understand.'

Using breaks to enhance learning

When we were born, we were unwittingly enrolled in two loyalty 'clubs'. Both clubs grant points to their members, and both offer appropriate rewards when points are accumulated.

The first club is called the 'brain break club'. The body has many rhythms. One is called our circadian rhythm, and approximates to the 24 hour clock. Other rhythms are called ultradian (more than daily) rhythms. Many of these are on a 90

The optimal period for learning.

minute cycle. It is interesting, therefore, to discover that the optimal period for learning is half of this cycle; 45 minutes. By taking a brain break every 45 minutes we maximize two friends of memory: primacy and recency. Primacy is remembering first things. Recency is remembering last things. For example, we have a tendency to remember first events and last events, such as the things on the top of our shopping list or things at the end, or our first day on a new job and the last day on an old job. This is also an interesting link to the importance of the first and last four minutes of any learning experience.

If we take regular brain breaks, we can cash in our points for prizes such as greater focus, new ideas, a boosted immune system, a better emotional state and more satisfying sleep.

The second club is called the 'brain breakdown club'. Members of this club collect points every time they choose not to take a break every 45 minutes. Bonus points are available to those who come into work early, work through lunch and leave late. Triple points are currently available for all members who work in the evenings as well, and serious collectors can be considered for platinum membership if they consistently work on their days 'off'.

Of course, the more points you collect, the greater the payback. Gold club level members can often enjoy tension headaches, emotional outbursts and regular periods of forgetfulness. Platinum club level members can even arrange for their immune systems to bail on them when they finally take some time off.

The above may have a humorous tone, but it is deadly serious. Taking brain breaks is not an option: it is an issue. It is not an alternative: it is an ultimatum. It is an organizational imperative if we want to build sustainable Living Organisations® – and is certainly one of the most simple steps individuals can take towards mental and emotional well-being.

Brain breaks can be managed using a simple kitchen timer.

MODELLING BRAIN BREAKS

During all the phases of delivering an Accelerated Training event, we use a simple kitchen timer set at 45 minute intervals. When it rings, we finish the point and take a 4 minute break. I even use this method when working from home, but when I am working on my own only a 2 minute break is necessary.

DISCOVERING INSIGHTS IN THE GAP

I have discovered a surprise benefit of this regular habit of taking short brain breaks in that there has been an increase in my personal creative output. It is usually 'in the gap' when an idea or a solution will present itself from my brain-in-the-basement to my fanatic-in-the-attic. Most of the time, the fanatic takes up all our attention. When we quieten the mind during a break time, the brain-in-the-basement can have the space necessary to get a thought up into consciousness.

Summary

Our second step, the 'Entrance' phase, is all about *making sense*. The designer of the learning and development experience is continually asking the question, 'How can I make my point in a way that stimulates as many senses as possible, in as rich a style as possible?' Subtle differences in the finer sensory distinctions (for example size, location, frequency, intensity, movement) make all the difference to the impact of the presentation of fresh or new ideas and information.

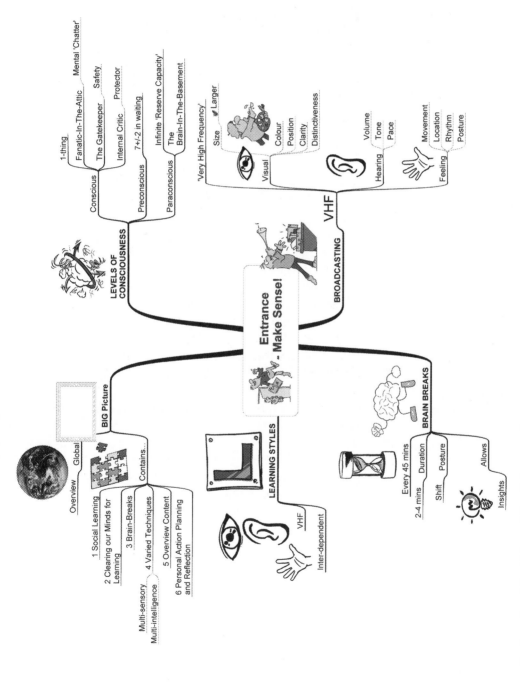

Figure 5 A review Mind Map of the Entrance phase

Switch OwNership – *Make it Intelligible!*

Switch OwNership is about facilitating learners to take control of how they make the new information personal.

How does the learning fit?

We have at least Seven Magnificent Intelligences . . . which learners use to make concepts *intelligible*.

If learners are to really apply their new learning, they will need to personalize or 'own' the learning. They will take the learning and frame it in a way that matches their own context. If the learning is to become habit, it will need to 'fit' until it becomes second nature to them. 'Second nature' is, of course, a cliché we use when something comes naturally.

We are making a distinction between the Entrance phase and the Switch OwNership phase. The Entrance phase is solely to do with the presentation of new or fresh information. The Switch OwNership phase begins the process of integration of material that has now been encountered. Since we take information in through our senses, the catchphrase for the Entrance phase is *'making sense!'*. However, during the Switch OwNership phase, we use the existing resources of our own intelligence to convert the learning into our own experience. This application of intelligence, we call *'making intelligible'*.

Howard Gardner of Harvard University has helped

us enormously by suggesting a model of multiple intelligence. Just as we are all on different wavelengths in terms of tuning-in to new information (VHF), so also we are very different when we deep process that information until it becomes fully intelligible to us, and thus a natural part of our repertoire.

Gardner originally suggested seven intelligences: mathematical/logical; linguistic; visual/spatial; physical; intrapersonal; interpersonal and musical. Both Gardner and Tony Buzan have added to or reframed this list since Gardner's original publication, *Frames of Mind*, and this has created some useful distinctions. However, I have found the original seven to be quite sufficient for facilitating the transfer of ownership. The 'how' is perhaps more important than the 'what'. And as Peter Thomson, the motivational speaker, says, 'Action *is* the key.'

Just as we have a sensory preference, we will also have a natural tendency to favour some intelligences over others.

When we help learners to switch on their multiple intelligences and apply this to the new learning, we allow the desired transfer of ownership. This then becomes intelligent training.

To achieve our outcome we merely orchestrate a sequence of activities that will require the application of each intelligence by the learners if they are to successfully tackle each activity. For example, if we were to ask a group to *estimate* or *calculate* the cost of implementing a business solution, this could not be achieved without switching on mathematical/logic intelligence. This takes us back to our ancient proverb: 'I hear, I forget; I see, I remember; I do, I understand'. The Switch OwNership phase is very much about 'doing'.

To 'do' anything, we must apply intelligence:
'I hear, I forget; I see, I remember; I do, I understand.'

mathematical-logical

linguistic

visual-spatial

Physical

Intrapersonal

Interpersonal

Defining the intelligences

Before we can design a strategy to activate these intelligences, it would be useful to be able to agree on a description and give an example of a possible profession for each one.

Mathematical/logical intelligence is the ability to work with numbers and reason to produce an outcome or recognize the structure and benefits of a line of thought. Simply put, it is skill with numbers and reasoning. *Accountant.*

Linguistic intelligence is the ability to articulate ideas in our own language. Simply put, it is skill with words and semantics. *Author.*

Visual/spatial intelligence is the ability to think visually and in three dimensions. Put simply, it is the ability to visualize concepts and the spatial relationships between concepts. *Architect.*

Physical intelligence is the ability to use our musculature and physical awareness to get the results we want. Put simply, it is the ability to manipulate physical objects to represent or achieve an outcome. *Athlete.*

Intrapersonal intelligence is the ability to 'go inside' and make connections. Put simply, it is the ability to make associations between what already exists in our experiential database and new experiences; to assign meanings or significance to these new experiences and to evaluate their worth. *Poet.*

Interpersonal intelligence is the ability to relate to other people with a view to sharing or clarifying or confuting the area under examination. Simply put, it is skill with people. *Nurse.*

Musical intelligence is the ability to articulate ideas and emotions through music. Simply put, it is skill with music. *Singer.*

Musical

Once we are comfortable with these definitions we can begin to plan how to switch them on, and in so doing, Switch OwNnership.

If you were to take some time aside now to think about the *verbs* that would activate each of these intelligences when asking a learner to complete a particular exercise, this would help you own this learning. Go back over each intelligence and list seven verbs that would necessitate the switching on of each of the magnificent seven intelligences. To help you, an example is given of each one.

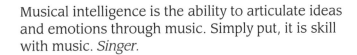

Mathematical/ Logical	Linguistic	Visual/Spatial	Physical	Intrapersonal	Interpersonal	Musical
Calculate	Write	Draw	Model	Reflect	Discuss	Compose
1.	1.	1.	1.	1.	1.	1.
2.	2.	2.	2.	2.	2.	2.
3.	3.	3.	3.	3.	3.	3.
4.	4.	4.	4.	4.	4.	4.
5.	5.	5.	5.	5.	5.	5.
6.	6.	6.	6.	6.	6.	6.
7.	7.	7.	7.	7.	7.	7.

Figure 6   Multiple intelligence table

Once you have generated your own list, the following give further examples of each intelligence to help you.

Mathematical/logical intelligence is switched on every time we calculate, reason, estimate, prioritize, create goals or objectives, generate lists, support our case with a rationale, justify our position, or add, subtract, multiply and divide.

Linguistic intelligence is switched on every time we articulate our ideas (or someone else's) in our own words. Writing, rewriting, describing, translating, rhyming, talking, acting and composing all involve linguistic intelligence. You may notice that we are already straying into other intelligences – musical for composing and rhyming, and both interpersonal (talking) and intrapersonal (thinking). This will be of great service to us, as trainers, later on because we will want to use combination activities that switch on more than one intelligence at a time.

Visual/spatial intelligence is switched on every time we make a spatial connection between objects or concepts. Drawing, sketching, colouring, Mind Mapping, flowcharting, 'PinPointing', painting, visualizing, imagining and daydreaming are all ways of connecting with this intelligence.

Physical intelligence is switched on every time we use movement to learn something. Dancing, walking, building, modelling, constructing, manipulating, moulding and making things are all catalysts for this intelligence. Any kind of 'hands-on' activity will serve us well here.

Certain groups of intelligences flow naturally together, and intrapersonal intelligence is usually the first we use.

Intrapersonal intelligence is switched on every time we 'go inside' and make connections. Meditating, reflecting, associating, imagining, critiquing, 'thinking', judging, evaluating, valuing and questioning all help build this intelligence. Asking someone for their opinion is a great way to release this intelligence with its partners: linguistic and logical intelligence.

Interpersonal intelligence is switched on any time you put people together and they communicate – even non-verbally. Discussing, arguing, sharing, debating, listening, presenting, defending, partying, playing in a team and reaching consensus will all strengthen this intelligence.

Musical intelligence is switched on every time we make an association between music and an emotional state, or a learning concept. This can be passive or active. Passive stimulation would include generating a list of songs that summarized a concept; a theme-tune approach. Active stimulation would include composing your own verses to a well-known tune, or writing a song from scratch. Karaoke can be the trainer's friend here. Utilizing rhythm, harmony, rhyme and melody can all accentuate this intelligence as can the good old-fashioned activity of musical appreciation.

When training 'live', we will rarely have time to dedicate to each intelligence sequentially. Instead, we will seek to switch on more than one intelligence with each activity. At the *design* stage, we would do well to work through planning how we will switch on each and every intelligence; giving us multiple opportunities of Switching OwNership.

Putting it together intelligently

ction

In the context of a training event, the programme designer can usefully sit down with a list of verbs and apply them to a sequence of activities that will move learners through the full complement of intelligences.

Here is an example for you to try:

1. Pause and reflect upon what you have learned so far. Pay special attention to action points you intend to take (intrapersonal intelligence backed up by logical).

2. Prioritize your learning and/or action points until you are happy with the seven most important learning points or actions (mathematical/logical).

3. Create a visual representation of the material you have learned, ideally showing the links between concepts. A Mind Map or visual representation, using your own words and images would be a great idea (visual/spatial backed up by interpersonal).

4. Choose a theme-tune or sound bite for each of your key points (musical intelligence.)

5. Imagine time stretching out around you. Decide where your first action or learning point is in physical space around you. Stand in this space and imagine yourself succeeding in applying this learning. Pay special attention to what you can see, hear and feel as you 'live' this memory of the future (physical and visual/spatial and intrapersonal intelligence).

6. Find someone whose opinions you value and share your discoveries with them (interpersonal intelligence).

YOUR DEVELOPMENT AS A TRAINER

One of the traps we, as trainers, can fall into is to play to our own strengths. Consider the seven intelligences and assess your own strengths and weaknesses. Since the mind works by associative logic and is synergistic, we can safely say that any attention you give to your weaker intelligences will have a disproportionately positive pay-off. If you strengthen your weaker areas, your stronger areas will also be enhanced by association.

Summary

During the 'Switch OwNership' phase we move to a more learner-directed style. The core attitudes, skills and knowledge have all been presented during the 'Entrance' phase, but there has been no transfer of ownership or control.

As learners take ownership and grow their own learning, we are not surprised that what comes up does not look like what we sowed!

Learners take control and ownership by applying their own portfolio of intelligences to the planted seed, allowing it to grow. However, as any gardener or farmer knows – what comes up rarely looks like what was sown! The learners may articulate what they have discovered in ways you would never have thought of. In this way they 'reframe' the learning to suit their own understanding.

Our role during this phase is to ensure sufficient activities and time to allow each intelligence to be applied to the key learning material – whether that be attitudes, skills or knowledge.

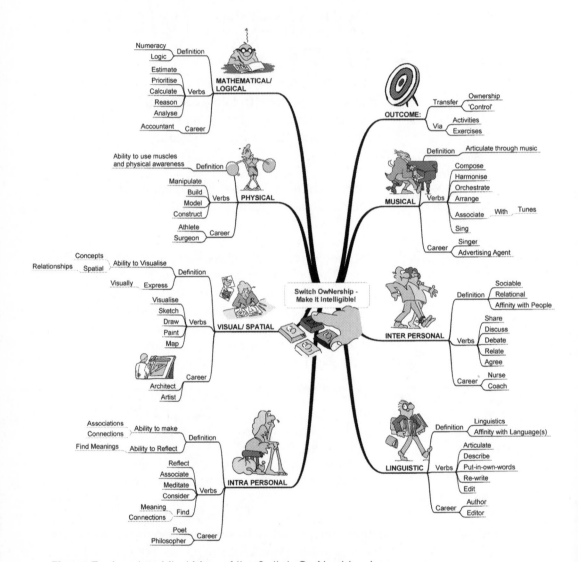

Figure 7 A review Mind Map of the Switch OwNership phase

PHASE FOUR

Store – *Make it Stick!*

Clearly, there is no point in investing vast amounts of time and energy in learning if we cannot then recall the learning.

Stephen Covey has some excellent insights on how we cannot cheat the system long-term. I, like Covey, cheated the system short-term. I discovered that I was able to load sufficient information into my short-term memory to pass an exam *if* I read through the key notes three times in close succession just before the exam. Now, however, years later, I have no access to that information I spent years of my life 'learning'. I did not know what I did not know – and one of the things I did not know was a strategy for taking the learning and moving it from short-term to long-term memory. I did not set out to 'cheat' the system, but I ended up being cheated by my own system!

Sustainable crops take months of nurturing. We shall mirror part of this process when we examine review during the 'Engage' phase. For now, let us examine how identifying and codifying key ideas will help us recall all our learning by *association*.

You cannot 'cheat' and 'beat' the system!

Hierarchies

Tony Buzan's Mind Mapping has to be the single greatest technique I have come across for getting my thinking clear and straight. As a thought-organizing tool, it works well for capturing fresh information, clarifying existing information, communicating clarified information and creating new combinations of information that lead to innovation.

The technique has its roots in memory principles. This is why we are introducing the 'how to' of the technique here. Fundamental to the approach is the ability to edit and recognize the hierarchies or levels of ideas.

Hierarchies or levels of ideas

Let's illustrate this with an example. Not all animals are the same. Some may be carnivores, some herbivores, some omnivores. However, all carnivores are animals, as are all herbivores. In this instance, 'animals' is at a higher or more general level of detail than 'omnivores'. In a similar way, once we have learned and personalized new information, we will begin to notice the hierarchies of ideas – the general categories and the supporting levels of detail that more specifically define the distinctions. This is important because it is the higher general groupings that we will want to codify as the first memory recall triggers. Tony Buzan calls these most general headings 'basic ordering ideas'.

For example:
Animals
   Herbivores
   Carnivores
   Omnivores
or:
Chapter heading
   Sub-heading

An example would be the M.E.S.S.A.G.E.™ model mnemonic. This mnemonic is a recall code for the highest and most general categories of what we are exploring in this publication; Mindset, Entrance, Switch OwNership, Store, Act, Go-Again, and Engage. These are broad headings that have very many levels of supporting detail beneath them. Yet, even with our exploration unfinished, you are well able to recall key ideas under the first three of these headings. Furthermore, the only trigger you initially need is the mnemonic. The

Like Russian dolls, key ideas have the supporting detail 'nested' within.

mnemonic has the other information 'nested' within it, just like Russian dolls.

Mindset, Entrance, Switch OwNership, Store, Act, Go-Again, and Engage are the basic ordering ideas of our approach.

When we have integrated the new learning on any subject into our own terms during the Switch OwNership Phase, we are then ready to edit the concepts and arrange them into a basic order or hierarchy of ideas. The top of each 'directory tree' can then be built into a memory device such as a poster, mnemonic, rhyme, song, sketch, rap, acrostic, flash cards, memory journey, link system, peg system, or Mind Map – or even a T-shirt.

How to Mind Map

Figure eight is an overview of core principles of Mind Mapping. Let us explore the 'hows', 'whys' and 'benefits' of this technique, and, in the process, uncover key principles for natural success in any area of our lives and learning.

I can only give you a brief outline of the skill, but if you find this introduction useful, we dedicate whole workshops to the application of the technique and software applications.

I am right-handed and all the right-handed Mind Mappers (or cerebral cartographers) I know mind map in a clockwise direction. Many of the left-handed Mind Mappers I know map in an anticlockwise direction. My belief is that habit is the mother of permanence. Habit can help our memory but can also lock us in from discovering new and wonderful experiences. Life is often about maintaining useful habits, and generating excellent new habits that will move us forwards. With Mind Mapping, I have found starting in the same place each time to be a useful habit for me. Looking at Figure 8, I started at one o'clock on the Mind Map

Figure 8 Overview of the core principles of Mind Mapping

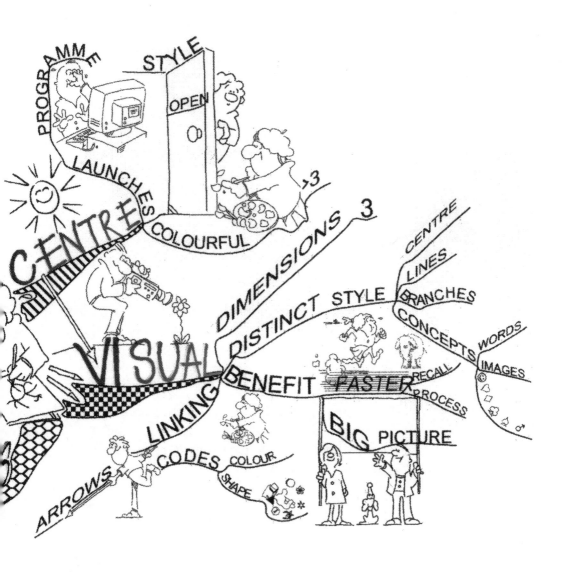

and then worked round clockwise. This would be a good way to read my map.

THE 'CENTRE'

The first chapter heading is 'centre'. Looking at the very centre of this map, you will notice that it is a visual image, unique to this map or to this concept. If I am cross-referencing this map to other areas I am learning, having a recurring image really helps consistent recall. I like to think that the mind has a 'desktop' like an Apple Mac computer or PC. On the 'desktop' of our mind we arrange our icons of what is important to us. Some of us may externalize this desktop in our work and home areas – perhaps with pictures or ornamentations that represent what is important to us.

Using an Apple computer or PC is easy *if* all the desktop icons are *distinct* – at a glance we can see where our favourite programmes are. What they look like and *where* they are is very important. I recently rearranged my icons by mistake and, although the icons remained the same, their *location* had changed. Even with a very limited screen size, I still found it hard to find my *favourites*. One of Mind Mapping's secrets to natural success is the position and style of the *central launch icon*. Our brain learns to look for the natural focal point of the page – the centre. If this centre is distinct for each subject area or application, it is very easy to launch the mental application software.

On this map, we have a woman drawing Mind Maps® – a simple summary of the key idea: 'how to make Mind Maps®'.

Let us follow the chapter heading 'Centre' through to its sub-headings. We can see now that the central image launches the programme or thinking application. It both opens the programme *and* benefits from an 'open', borderless style. We all walk through life in thinking bubbles. How big our bubble is defines the expansive nature of our

Your central image should be free of any frame or boundary so that it is visibly connected to the ideas that radiate out from it.

thoughts and possibilities. Once we lock an idea in a bubble; even on a page, we restrict its expansive nature. Keep your central image free of a boundary; no frame, no border, just open. This helps each central icon be distinct because using frames is a great way to add emphasis. So, let us keep this emphatic tool for highlighting anything remarkable that comes up elsewhere in the map.

This publication has remained largely in black and white so that it remains commercially viable. However, wherever possible we strongly recommend the use of *more than three colours* to add distinctiveness. On this map, we have used an alternative form of distinctiveness; shaded branches. This is particularly useful if there is any degree of colour blindness. The key outcome is distinctiveness.

THE 'VISUAL' BRANCH

We have about 96 per cent recall of distinctive visuals. This means that making our environment or our Mind Map visually rich gives us a 96 per cent chance of recalling the key information. We even say, 'A picture is worth a thousand words.'

There are many ways to enrich our map visually. Using dimension appeals to a stronger preference of the right hemisphere of the brain. Many of us 'doodle' when we are on the phone. We draw geometric shapes, make them look like they are 3D, and then colour them in. This is because the telephone call is either not engaging enough or else we are an habitual fiddler. With Mind Mapping, we can harness this habit for learning. Didactic Doodles! The way we do this is beautifully simple; just make the doodles mean something.

Your style is important. Be yourself, and be distinctive. Your brain likes you! It does not matter if you 'cannot draw'. All you have to be able to do is recognize what your scratches on the paper mean. Develop a distinctive way of using lines and

The rhinencephalon, or 'nose brain' is the centre for emotional responses, long-term recall and learning. As the name might suggest, it is strongly influenced by smell.

branches. Develop your own style for each central image. Conceptualize your thoughts in visual words, images and icons.

What are the benefits of visual thinking? Sight is the fastest sense to be *consciously* processed by the mind. (Smell seems to be the fastest, sense to be processed by the other-than-conscious-mind – going straight to the emotional, long-term recall and learning centres of the brain, the rhinencephalon.)

With visual thinking being a faster process and with faster recall, it is a key to thinking faster, not harder. Natural success comes from visual thinking. Great thinkers throughout history have painted word pictures for us, or even literal paintings and works of art to capture our imagination. Seeing *is* believing: if we can see something in our mind's eye, then we can believe it.

Visual thinking also helps us to get the BIG Picture overview, giving us a sense of comfort when we can see the context for what we are trying to learn and understand. When we have the BIG picture for our lives, we feel we are pretty much on top of things; we know where we are going and there is comfort in that. Having the BIG picture of any subject we are learning helps us feel like we have the lid of the jigsaw puzzle to guide us as we piece the details together.

With visual thinking being faster for both processing ideas and recalling them, and great for the comfort of the BIG Picture, and for enhancing recall, isn't it about time you realized the artist inside?

A third key benefit is that of degree of recall. As I said above, we can have 96 per cent recall of visual imagery. So, do art!

Finally, in our consideration of visual mapping, we do well to map out our associations by showing links with arrows or with codes, perhaps using colours or shapes. Mind Maps® are fantastic for mapping complexity and then for navigating our way through complex adaptive systems. By using land*markers* along the journey, we can see the connections within each thinking model we explore. This is also a commercial benefit, since we can often notice where there is duplication of effort, or a better way of getting from A to B. This way, we can improve quality and cut costs.

Have a go at designing a central image for the following subjects: time management, work/life balance and project management.

THE 'CONCEPTS' BRANCH

On this branch we explore some of the key concepts of Buzan's Mind Mapping.

You may be familiar with the K.I.S.S. principle? 'Keep it short and simple.' Mind Mapping is very much about editing. You edit your own and other people's ideas using your *own* words, images and concepts. This way, you *own* the learning. You also let go of the destructive force of perfectionism; needing to get down every word just right. It's time to get a life and think for ourselves!

Use the K.I.S.S. principle *and* emotion to make each Mind Map personal to you and powerfully memorable.

Linking to kissing is the concept of emotivity. We know that the emotional centre of the brain is linked inextricably to long-term memory recall and to learning; therefore, if we make our maps emotive they will stick in our mind. Usually this means having fun whilst you map out the thoughts. However, I do recognize that some subjects are not fun, for example, dealing with bereavement, *but they are meaningful and are thus emotive.* For example, one of my best lecturers at college irritated and annoyed me because he challenged my comfort zone and yet his classes were very emotive and meaningful, even if I did not find them fun.

Another concept is that of using images. I hope you can see how I have iconically cross-referenced 'faster', 'recall' and 'colour' from this section to other areas in the map. Have another look and see if you can spot the similar images.

Images enable us to recall vast amounts faster. They are also the best way to code vast amounts of information. Images can also be emphatic; by deliberate use of colour, highlighting and outlining.

Words are also valuable, especially when we use visual onomatopoeia. Using key words only allows us to save time and space, leaving us more time to think for ourselves. Sensory words directly trigger our senses, so they literally 'make more sense'. Abstract words are not sensory, and can become 'non-sense'. Printed words help us clearly take in what is on the whole Mind Map in one glance: almost a photographic memory. We are seeking visual clarity and impact.

Onomatopoeia!

What does onomatopoeia mean? It means a word that sounds like the concept it is representing, for example, 'Bang!' A great way to expand your visuality is to develop 'visual onomatopoeia' – words that look like the concept they are representing. Just see how easy the following are to decode:

1. ☺ut
2. GROWING
3. LINE
(1 = 'time out'; 2 = 'growing'; 3 = 'underline')

This means that if you cannot think of an image to represent an idea, there may be a way of making the very word itself look like the concept.

You may also notice on this map that there are no phrases or sentences. Each word is on its own line. This strict principle enables each phrase to be broken open to form new associations; rather like the DNA double helix opening up to generate new life. Keep to the principle 'one word per line' for your first one hundred Mind Maps®, and see how it works for you.

THE 'COLOUR' BRANCH

The key benefits of using colour are that it is fun and distinctive and it also leads to a 50 per cent boost in likelihood of recall. Any executive who frowns at your use of coloured pens may be freed from their thinking bubble by informing them of the 50 per cent boost in mental performance through the use of colour. Colour your life! I am horrified at how grey some offices and fashions are.

Colour benefits from being used systematically and consistently. It is not colour for colour's sake. We can use colour to bring order to a black and white map; perhaps showing the priorities for learning or action. We can use colour to codify subject areas. We can also use colour to emphasize areas of special interest that emerge through the thinking process.

A completed Mind Map may appear chaotic at first glance, as indeed does the structure of the brain. This chaos is an illusion. There is a clear ordering of ideas on a well-structured map.

THE 'STRUCTURE' BRANCH

Chapter headings are clearly linked to the central image and both the size of their font and the width of their supporting branch shows the size of the information they are organizing. They are the BIG ideas, and very general. The supporting twigs and ideas are clearly different because of size, connectivity and position on the page.

Lines show the connectivity of all ideas, allowing ideas to flow like impulses down the axons of each neuron. The connected lines reflect the architecture we find in nature; natural architecture. They are organic, soft and flowing, they literally 'underline' every thought and act as 'guidelines'.

No Mind Map is an island. There is an ocean of forgetfulness 'out there' that is the greatest threat to the Store phase of our model. Within that ocean there are many hazards to distract us from accurate recall. We need to connect our Mind Maps® to our daily habits so that our insights remain in-sight, in-mind. To do this we can use a memory rhythm. This is the mirror image of the preview build up we mentioned during the Mindsetting phase, and it will be dealt with in detail during our Engage phase (see later). However, suffice to say here that we can safeguard the learning encoded in our Mind Map – our treasure map – if we review our Mind Map (or any memory device) within the first 5–10 minutes after learning, within the first hour (code 60), the first day (code 24), the first week (code 7), the first month (code 31) and at the three month stage (code 93).

Have a go now at exploring one of the concepts in this publication so far using a Mind Map.

Five core principles of memory

Five keys to all memory systems are:
○ **a**ssociation
○ **e**mphasis
○ **i**magination
○ **o**rder
○ **u**nusual.

Associations anchor new information to the already familiar.

All memory systems work on five common core principles. I call these the 'vowels of memory'. A is for **a**ssociation. We can only learn and memorize concepts that we can associate with. Associations are like hooks, and to make a message stick, it must have as many hooks as possible on it. The conductor of the Boston Philharmonic Orchestra, Benjamin Zander, transformed my attitude to the music of the composer, Mahler. Before I heard Zander's lecture on the life of Mahler, I had found the music impenetrable; I had no associations with it. After Zander explained how the 6th Symphony was a reflection of Mahler's life story, the music became accessible and valued.

Association is the key to every memory system I know. The art is to take something that is fixed and familiar in the memory, and then attach the information to be recalled. For example, a process with a clear sequence can be associated with a familiar journey. Golfers who need to memorize the function keys (F1 – F12) for a software programme can easily recall each unique function by associating them with the first 12 holes of their favourite golf course.

Movement is more memorable.

E is for **e**mphasis. Adding emphasis gives more 'charge' to what we want to memorize. Emphasis can be added through making the material emotive, or erotic, or exaggerated, or 'energetic' through movement. For example, it is easy to remember a monkey and a racing car. However, imagining a monkey driving a racing car is far more memorable.

Capture the imagination.

I is for **i**magination. Any time we capture someone's imagination, we have embedded a concept in their memory. To empower our participants to be able to recall, we must allow them to stimulate their own imaginations. Imagination is more powerful than willpower. Think how many times you have changed your mind after a period of imagination.

Anything ordered or sequenced in patterns is easy to remember.

O is for **o**rder. Anything that is presented in a logical sequence is far easier to recall. This is because we can follow the chain of associations, link by link.

Finally, U is for **u**nusual. Anything unusual sticks in the mind and can assist recall. The really amazing fact is that the unusual experience does not have to be directly related to the learning. So, for example, holding a training event in an unusual location will help it stick in the learners' minds. Once, a labrador walked into my history lesson at school. This had nothing to do with world history, but the event was totally unique and unusual. The result has been that I can still remember that lesson, and that we were studying the Strait of Magellan, even though it was 26 years ago! My excellent history teacher, Mrs Mahoney, did not make a link between the dog and the lesson. She did not need too, the message stuck because of the unusual event. This concept can be combined powerfully with the importance of the 'first four minutes'. Orchestrating something unusual in the first or last four minutes of your learning experience can ensure that the key points stick forever!

Labradors – the secret of recall for 26 years?

ction

Think of a forthcoming meeting or training event. How could you build associations between your key messages for this event and the other attendees' experience? What could you do to emphasize key points? How could you capture your audience's imagination? How could you establish a clear order or sequence to the message that needs to be conveyed? What could you do that would be so unusual that it would make the meeting or event stand out in people's minds?

Summary

Whichever memory tools you use during this phase, we know they all work by association and benefit from regular review. Adding emphasis, imagination, order and the unusual will make the memory imprinting even more effective. Making your life and environment visually rich and colourful, noticing the links between ideas and learning to reframe ideas in your own thoughts are all great ways to develop a rich memory as a resource to get more out of life and learning. As a trainer, during this phase you will help the learners construct the most appropriate method for them to store their treasured learning and to find it again later!

This can be through Mind Mapping, or through memory systems such as stories, poems or raps, or through building associations with items that are already fixed in the memory.

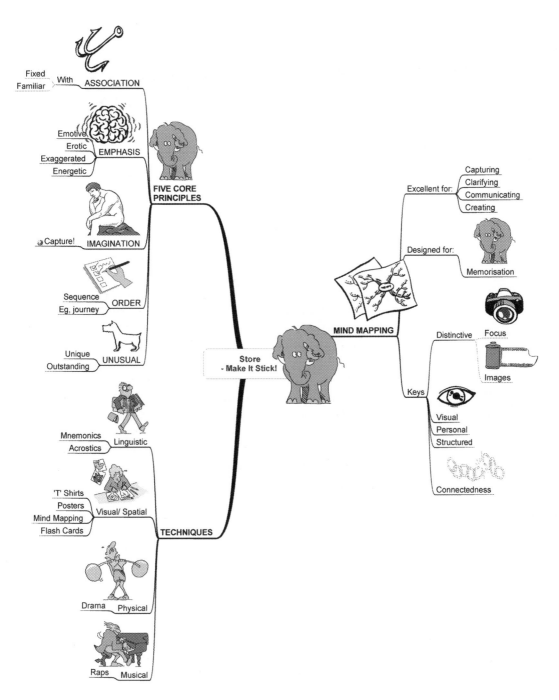

Figure 9 A review Mind Map of the Store phase

Act – *Make it Show!*

Act is about giving the learners an opportunity to demonstrate their new skills or knowledge. *Make it Show!*

When we catch ourselves doing something right, it increases our confidence and our competence. The 'Act' phase focuses on designing space for the learners to demonstrate competence and so build confidence. It is also about learners demonstrating to themselves the relevance of the learning.

Our purpose is twofold: to boost each participant's confidence, and to verify competence.

For the trainer, it allows us to test whether our broadcasting of the key messages has been successful. If not, we then have the opportunity to adjust our approach, returning to the Entrance, Switch OwNership and Store phases of the model until our learners demonstrate competence at the Act phase.

Formats for the Act phase

For skills-based learning, the Act phase can readily take the form of a demonstration of the desired skill. For more conceptual learning, we can enjoy testing knowledge in the form of a low-threat, yet high-energy 'game show'. This has become a firm favourite in my workshops and has improved my own enjoyment of delivering training.

ction

How are you doing?

Let us now practice this phase of the model. See how well you are doing so far through filling out the following crossword. The outcome is to catch-yourself-getting-it-right, which means that you are welcome to review your notes, or scan the book after you have seen whether the answer leaps to mind.

Clues Across

1. By using the principle of 'the more ways you teach, the more people you reach' we may be said to be doing this activity as used by radio and TV stations.
5. What device can be used during the Store phase to aid memory recall?
6. The objects of our desire.
8. No Mind Map is one of these.
9. You only have four of these to make an impact.
11. An off-shoot of growing competence.
14. Ninety-six percent of this is available if you use visuals.
15. What sort of stimuli will impact on the other-than-conscious mind?
16. An architecture favoured and reflected in Mind Maps®.
18. What happens to anything you pay attention to in your awareness?
19. The wavelength that everyone tunes in to.
20. What is gained by keeping matters 'in-mind'?
21. The popular name for the rhinencephalon.
23. The things you are seeking to stimulate and build during the Mindset phase.
24. Three letter summary for the wavelength that makes sense.
25. Influences that we would do well to park, put in the dustbin or store in a safe place.

Clues Down

1. That which does us good every 45 minutes.
2. Using this during Mind Mapping appeals to a preference of the right hemisphere of the brain.
3. The brain waves preferred for deep integration.
4. The intelligence used to work out the answers to this.
7. Which type of thinking is faster for both processing ideas and recalling them?
10. The first intelligence to be used . . . usually!
12. The purpose of putting learning on any subject into our own terms.
13. The establishment of a rhythmic relationship or a frequency following response.
17. The very thing you are trying to demonstrate during this phase.
22. The brain waves favoured for learning new information.

(Answers in Appendix A at the back of the book.)

Other activities for the Act phase

Other types of activities that work well during the Act Phase include team challenges and connecting grid games.

With a team challenge, split your delegates into the group size of your choice. Ask each team to review the learning and to come up with your chosen number of questions for the other team. You can set more questions than needed. This precludes the problem of duplicate questions and also encourages more review!

Each team asks questions in turn, and points are awarded depending on whether the question is answered or not. If a team gets the answer right, they get a set number of points. If they cannot answer the question, and you think it is a fair question, the questioning team gets bonus marks.

Connecting grid games illustrate the principle of the importance of association. There is a version of the TV Show *Blockbusters* available as a game. This letter-based grid works brilliantly because you can be thinking up questions throughout the duration of the learning event. The game is then very definitely grounded in the learning experience of the day. The TV game, *Blockbusters*, uses a board made of connecting hexagons. The aim is for each team to form a line of connections from one side of the board to the other, or from top to bottom. Using normal alphabet letters, you can think up questions that test learning, and the letter on the board triggers the correct answer to the question.

With huge groups, it is possible to play table against table and still run a viable game show. A sample is provided below for you to try out and test your learning.

And here are the questions:

(answers in Appendix A at the back of the book)

Which 'A' is the communication that Accelerated Trainers use?

Which 'B' can Accelerated Trainers use to enhance learning?

Which 'C' can improve your memory recall by 50 per cent?

Which 'D' can be emphasized through shading?

Which 'E' represents the last part of the M.E.S.S.A.G.E.™ model of Accelerated Training?

Which 'F' would we do well to transform into benefits?

Which 'G' is a learning behaviour demonstrated by blue tits, but not by robins?

Which 'H' is an activity that will serve us well if under the physical intelligence area?

Which 'I' is the intelligence switched on when you ask people to discuss a point of view?

Which 'L' type recall is found in the rhinencephalon?

Which 'M' is the foundation of the M.E.S.S.A.G.E.™ model of Accelerated Training?

Which 'N' is a key preference of mathematical/logical Intelligence?

Which 'O' is beneficial if used for the centre of a Mind Map?

Which 'P' launches our P.O.W.E.R.F.U.L. mnemonic?

Which 'R' relates to this sequence: 5–10; 60; 24; 7; 31; 93?

Which 'S' belongs to learners in the M.E.S.S.A.G.E.™ model of Accelerated Training?

Which 'T' is a wave useful for deep integration?

Which 'U' is a key point to do with lines and words on a Mind Map?

Which 'V' in general are more effective, the larger and more colourful we make them?

Which 'W' describes WIIFM and VHF?

Summary

Your imagination is the key here. There are only two goals to achieve. Firstly, generate different ways to test the efficacy of your training. Secondly, make these ways entertaining so that your participants will have a pleasurable experience of catching themselves 'getting it right', making it show. Achieve these and you will have fulfilled all that is required during this fun phase of the M.E.S.S.A.G.E.™ model of Accelerated Training.

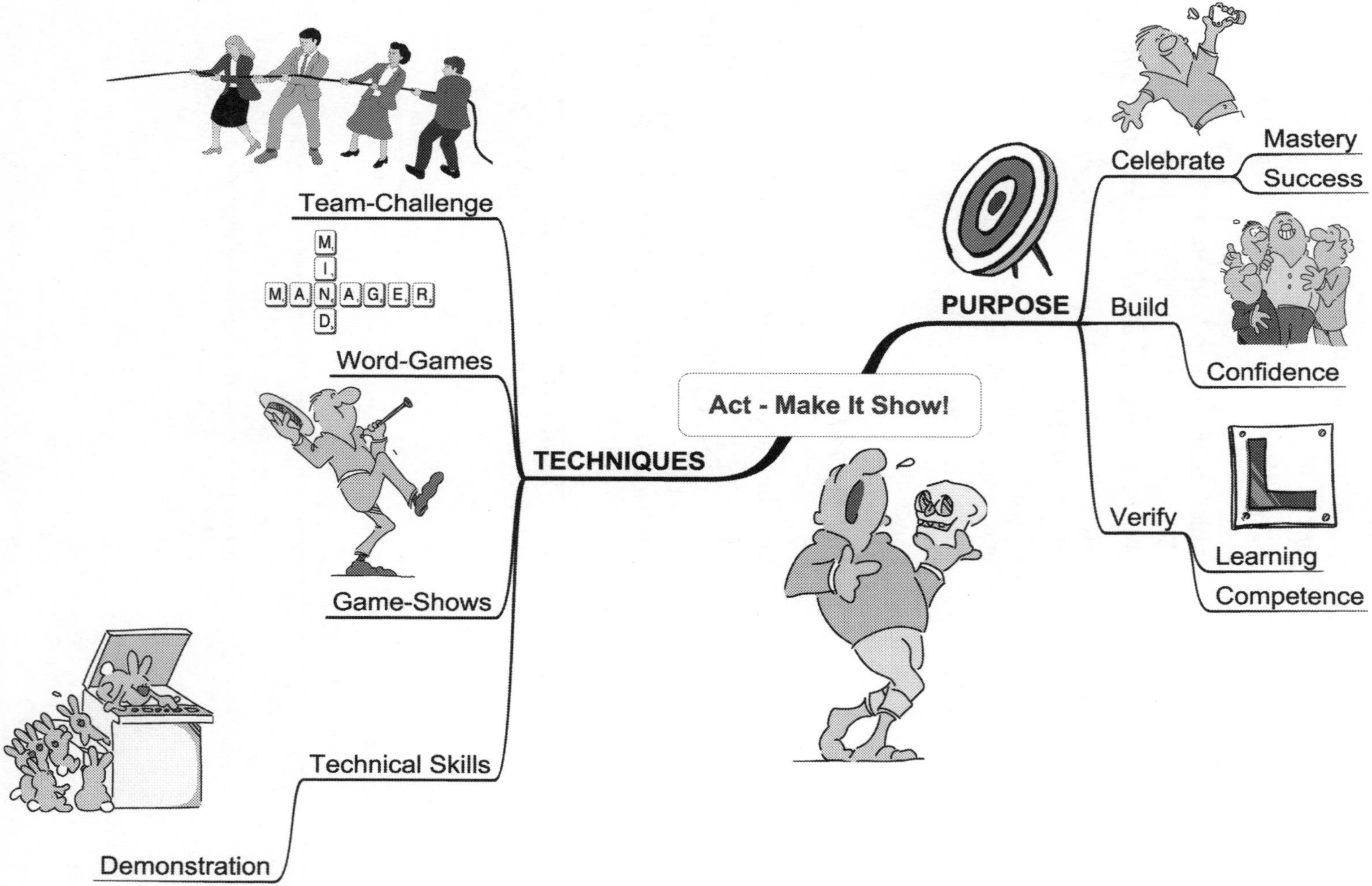

Figure 10 A review Mind Map of the Act phase

Going Again is about revisiting the learning journey to strengthen the sense of familiarity with the new material. The outcome is unconscious competence, the learning having become deeply assimilated to the point that it is 'second nature'. During this phase we want the learning to be so much a part of us that it naturally flows: *make it flow!*

PHASE SIX

Go-Again – *Make it Flow!*

There can be few pleasures as exhilarating as knowing that you have 'got it' or that you have 'got what it takes'. Having the answer on the tip of your tongue, even if you do not say it out loud, really feels good and boosts confidence.

This phase of the model is probably the most exciting for those of us who have been training for years, and also the least practised or understood. Why is this? Perhaps it is because this is the phase that is most unusual and beyond orthodox patterns of training and development. If delivered inexpertly, it can be misconstrued as 'off with the fairies' or 'new age'. I do not know what the problem with new age is, as most of the new age people I know are trying their best to make the world a better place. However, I do understand organizations' needs to be seen to be using training methods which have their feet on the ground even if their inspiration is above the clouds.

During this phase, we deliberately harness entrainment. Entrainment is developing a rhythmic relationship with something else, or a frequency following response. For example, as mentioned before, a baby that rests for long enough against its mother's breast will change its heartbeat to be in synchrony with its mother's heartbeat. When a couple are relaxed with each other, they will often find their breathing in harmony with one another, and when walking they will walk in perfect time.

When in harmony with others, synchronous walking and breathing are physical examples of entrainment; the natural mechanism that supports interpersonal intelligence.

Entrainment is the physical and mental outworking of the beauty of rapport. It is joining each other in the dance of life. This sounds all very 'nice' but the value to us in learning goes much deeper. It is possible to encourage learners to get into a state of mind where theta waves begin to predominate.

Theta waves are the waves associated with deep relaxation, to the point where you are just about asleep. In this state you can sometimes be unsure of which reality is real. For example, you may be convinced that you have put the cat out for the night, and then the cat leaps on to the bed. This sense of reality can be harnessed to help us make the learning more compelling to ourselves at the deepest levels of consciousness. The result is that we find ourselves acting upon our learning without thinking; a state we sometimes call 'unconscious competence'.

This phase is perhaps the key to skills and knowledge transfer at work and yet it is the one phase that tends to get dropped when the trainer lack self-confidence or is under time pressure. Why is this? It is because this phase is the least attractive to the busy fanatic-in-the-attic. During this phase we really do relax.

Some people even fall asleep, and this can seem like a luxurious use of limited training times. What I am going to suggest is that utilizing this phase is an economic imperative. If you sell the benefits of the deep integration and unconscious competence that become available, you will be able to get a positive response from your group.

I'm reviewing... honestly!

The deep review achieved during this phase can be so relaxing that people fall asleep. However, they can still review the material even though they are apparently tuned out.

The review concert

The review and active concerts were first devised by Georgi Lozanov.

This phase draws directly on the wonderful work of Georgi Lozanov. He uses two concerts in his training: an active concert during the equivalent of our Entrance phase, and a passive or review concert during the equivalent to this Go-Again phase. In practice, Lozanov runs the two concerts back to back, whereas in our case the Entrance phase and the Go-Again phase are widely separated. This is an alternative structure to the Lozanov method and should be recognized as such. During any active concert, the learners are fully outwardly focused on the *fresh* material they are assimilating for the first time. During any passive concert, the learners are progressively inwardly focused on the *already known and experienced* material. The goal is inward mastery.

The review concert technique is literally like a concert. The Lozanov method celebrates the metaphor of a classical concert because the state of mind of being physically relaxed, yet mentally attentive – as you would be at a classical concert – is the ideal state for deep absorption. Music is chosen that evokes the appropriate emotional state for deep review and reflection. The beat is very important since it will become the key frequency or rhythm to entrain the theta-dominant brain wave state. Sixty beats per minute appears to be ideal. The *largo* movements found in baroque music are often 60 bpm.

The facilitator *orchestrating* the review concert prepares an individual summary of the learning journey, personalizing it to each group wherever practical. The group then uses a technique such as Romen progressive relaxation (where we systematically check that each area of the body is relaxed) to access the state of 'body relaxed, mind awake'.

With the music *quietly* in the background, the conductor of the concert invites the group to 'go inside' and review their learning. It is important that the conductor-facilitator uses general terms so that the learner can fill in the details for themselves. This is because it is possible during a relaxation exercise for the facilitator to suggest something that is incongruent with the way a participant is thinking and the next thing they know is they are shocked out of their relaxed state. I remember this happening to me when we were asked to imagine a relaxing beach. The facilitator then suggested we

Like a classical concert, the review concert benefits from a state of body–mind where the body is comfortable and relaxed yet the mind is sharp and attentive. It is a superb example of the application of musical intelligence.

Relaxation exercises should be framed in general terms . . . being too specific can shock people out of a relaxed state because the image you suggest was not part of their reverie.

noticed the rock in the foreground. There was no rock on my beach until then, and its sudden appearance rather ruined the effect.

The most crucial aspect of the conductor's facilitation is the use of the voice. The voice must become like one of the instruments in the ensemble. This means that the conductor must moderate and vary the tone, volume and speed to pace the style and flow of the chosen musical performance. The voice merges with the music. Since the music is played quietly, the voice also must match the mood, yet remain clear and distinct.

Remember, the voice is a performance and, as such, should be dramatic, engaging the imagination and emotions. Build in a story-like structure, metaphors and parables wherever you can. This is far more appealing to all three levels of consciousness. Capturing the imagination of each member of the audience means that the attention is transfixed for short-term memory, whilst the story structure provides multiple hooks to trigger long-term memory recall.

You will have the benefit of learning from my mistakes. In the early days of assessing trainers for the award of the 'Certificate in Accelerated Training Practice', I would find that the innovators and early adopters who came on my first few programmes were wonderful enthusiasts. Almost without exception, their sensory learning preference was visual. They thought in pictures, they talked in pictures, they even walked like pictures, all arms and legs. This is their strength.

People who think in pictures have to race along with their speech in order to keep up with the rapidity of their thoughts. It's like thinking at the speed of light and trying to catch up at the speed of sound.

One of the by-products of thinking visually is the speed of your speech. If you think in pictures you have to accelerate your speaking to keep up with the rapid flow of thoughts through your mind. This often means that you talk at very high rates.

What I discovered was that our visually-focused trainers were so excited about what they had learned with each group that they forgot to keep their voice entrained at 60 bpm *on the first few attempts*. You can imagine what it is like to be told to relax by someone who is talking at 90 miles per hour!

How did we help our trainers learn to slow down and emphasize the beat? What has worked well for us is to use a metronome. We set the metronome to 60 bpm and then asked the facilitator to tap their foot in time to the beat whilst at the same time reading a favourite piece of poetry. It really does not take much practice 'off-line' to be able to develop the natural flexibility needed to entrain theta waves by slowing the pace of our delivery.

Using a metronome can help rapid talkers s-l-o-w down their pace to emphasize 60 bpm – thus entraining theta waves.

The next stage is then to exchange the metronome with a *largo* movement from a piece of baroque music that you enjoy and that relaxes you, because 'you' are the key. I encourage the facilitators to keep tapping along with the beat of the music and read some more poetry out loud. We have found this simple twofold development strategy to work very successfully.

The idea is to accentuate the beat, not talk mechanically like a zombie, robot, or mummy.

Perhaps it would be good for me to mention another trap you can avoid. When you practice this, and tap your feet first to the metronome and then to the music, do remember that you are only accentuating the beat – not talking to the beat. On rare occasions I have had delegates transformed into robots, zombies or mummies as they mechanistically emphasize each word . . . on . . . the . . . beat! I take full responsibility for this miscommunication on my behalf. The key point is that the beat receives attention, but it is fully acceptable to have moments where your voice moves quickly in a trill of notes around the beat. Just imagine that your voice is a lead melody line in the music which accentuates the beat with movement all around the beat.

The other excellent side-benefit from developing this new skill is that visually dominant people can learn to slow down and match the speed of other people when they are in a conversation with someone whose preference is other than visual. To an unrestrained or unretrained visual person, anyone talking at a slower rate may appear 'slow' or 'dim'. To someone who has a preference other than visual, listening to a visual person can be quite exhausting, the visual person appearing possibly 'flighty' or 'shallow'. So, greater rapport and behavioural flexibility all round can be gained by attention to this simple exercise of talking along to a metronome and then some *largo* movements from baroque music you like.

How to construct a review concert

Step 1:
Prepare your personal summary
of the learning journey.

Step 2:
Mind Map a rough route map to
give structure yet remain flexible.

Step 3:
Orchestrate the environment for
deep relaxation.

1. Prepare your summary of the learning journey. In private, reflect on the learning opportunities the learners have encountered sequentially from the advanced communication right through to the Act phase demonstration of their new discoveries.

2. Mind Map this as a rough route map. Whilst a script may be comforting to read from if you do not feel competent and confident, it will interfere with you noticing the vital clues given to you by your group. Mind Maps® give you far greater flexibility to lead the orchestration of this concert.

3. Adjust the environment to enhance the likelihood of deep relaxation. Some groups may even feel comfortable enough with you to feel free to lie on the floor. With senior executives who have been too busy to read their explanatory advance communication packs, I quickly remind them of how I was allowed to put my head down on the desk at junior school whilst the teacher introduced us to some of the great classics of literature. Most share this memory and so there is a comfortable sense of familiarity with what we then move on to do.

Step 4:
Begin the music.

Step 5:
Relaxation exercise.

Step 6:
Begin the journey.

Step 7:
Add positive suggestions.

Step 8:
Imagine the future applications.

Step 9:
S-l-o-w-l-y draw the groups attention to external stimuli.

4. Begin the music. The Lozanov method would suggest you add a sense of ceremony by mentioning the composer and the piece as if this were the introduction to a classical concert.

5. Undertake a short progressive relaxation exercise, and notice how the breathing of the group slows as they allow their physical body to deeply relax and begin to physically 'tune in' to the beat of the music.

6. Begin the review of the learning journey, helping them revisit in general terms the passage of their learning over time. Speaking in generalizations that must be true for the group puts participants' 'gatekeepers' at ease, and allows them to imagine their own specific details.

7. As the journey comes to an end, add some positive suggestions about how easy it is to act on what we know deep down inside to add colour to your generalizations. In a classical sense, this is pure 'allegory', where each element of the story of learning has a unique relevance for each learner's perceived reality.

8. Invite the still relaxed learners to let their attention drift into their future and notice where they will have the first opportunities to apply this learning. Ask them to remember these future cues that they can apply their new learning.

9. In case anyone has gone into a very deeply relaxed state, take a few moments to *slowly* begin to draw the group's attention to a more external focus. For example, 'As the time now draws nearer for us bring this part of our learning experience to a close, would you allow yourself to become more aware of

Step 10:
Group shares insights into how
they will apply the learning.

the sounds around you.' Pace the reality of the world around, for example any traffic noises in the distance, or the sound of the air conditioning; anything that *has* to be true if they focus externally. Then invite them to open their eyes if they were closed, to stretch and to share a smile with someone else in the group. Remind them that even with their eyes wide open they can be fully alert and yet still relaxed.

10. As we move into the final phase of the model, the Engage phase, I would then ask the group to share examples of the first few opportunities where they will be able to exercise their new discoveries.

The actual delivery of the Go-Again phase is rarely longer than 10 minutes, so there is every reason to include it in your training plan, and precious little excuse for excluding it! In contrast, the Lozanov method uses up to 90 minutes performance time for the combined active and passive Concerts.

ction

Practice musically 'surfing' your voice with the mood, pace and volume of your chosen pieces of music.

Practice

Practice in private first. Choose some favourite baroque *largo* movements. Get familiar with the ebb and flow of these pieces because when you join the orchestration you will seek to 'musically surf' these waves of mood, pace and volume. This matching of your delivery to the flow of the music marks the difference between amateur and professional delivery.

If possible, have some way of recording yourself. Have a simple story or set of poems to read. Start the recorder and introduce the music. Fade in the music, if the piece lends itself to a fade in.

Once the music is at an appropriate level, invite yourself to relax, perhaps by means of a brief progressive relaxation exercise. Ideally, imagine a group there with you and take them through the relaxation with you. When and **only** when you feel relaxed, begin reading your story or poems, over the music, at approximately the same volume.

When you've finished, pause, then begin, out loud, to draw your attention to external stimuli. Raise your voice slightly louder than the music as you come back to this reality. Fade out the music professionally.

Summary

Going Again is the key review phase of our model, strengthening the learning so powerfully that it becomes 'second nature'. Participants will find themselves applying the learning without having to think twice once the key learning is established as being deeply familiar at the most profound levels of consciousness.

To achieve this we orchestrate a learning integration experience that encourages a theta-dominant brain wave state; the state associated with deep reverie. We do this by combining music with a slow tempo (*largo* movements), and reviewing the learning with our narrative delivered in such a way that it 'surfs' along with the changes in the music's mood, pace and volume. In this way the voice and the music seem as one, and the 'reserve capacity' of the other-than-conscious mind is unlocked as 'unconscious competence'.

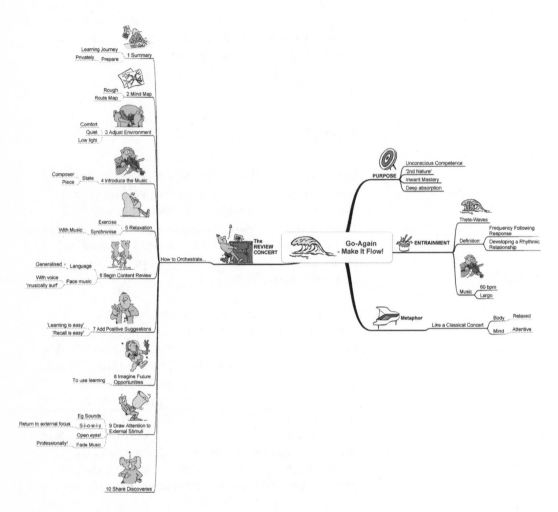

Figure 11 A review Mind Map of the Go-Again phase

PHASE SEVEN

Engage is about visiting the future and setting up a template for ensuring future success; it includes engaging commitment to an habitual review schedule that will ensure we keep our learning and develop it further evermore.

Engage – *Make it So!*

Here, at the close of the M.E.S.S.A.G.E.™ model of Accelerated Training, we will examine the power of developing memories of the future, the importance of review, and then apply the principle of engagement to developing your own design template for a forthcoming training or development event. We choose a future and *make it so!*

Memories of the future . . . imagining future practical scenarios, the process begun during the close of the review concert.

Memories of the future

David Ingvar of the University of Lund in Sweden tells us that the brain is a scenario-making mechanism. When we are asleep, and when we are awake, it is running multiple scenarios of 'what if . . .?' It takes the information we have available and associates it together (often in strange ways in dreams), then it extrapolates likely outcomes if we commit to a certain course of action. For example, you may be in a meeting and the thought comes to you, 'What if I caught a later train tonight?' Without needing to be asked, your brain will then run some of the likely consequences of catching that later train. You may get a seat? You may just have to get a 'take-away' instead of cooking? You could stay really late in town and see an old friend or a show.

Somewhere along the line, your emotions can become engaged too and a sense of commitment or buy-in to the new idea emerges.

This scenario then runs as a memory-resident programme and when data comes in via your senses that equates to part of your scenario, you become more consciously aware of the choice you made in principle. You can then decide whether or not to play out the scenario.

Even our imagined scenarios to do with potential futures are stored as memories – hence the phrase, 'memories of the future'.

The charming thing about Ingvar's research is his assertion that even though these scenarios are to do with the future and unseen, the only way they can be stored is as a memory *as if* they have happened as a reality. Hence his title for them, 'memories of the future'.

I sometimes call these 'temporal templates'. We then navigate our way through the complexities of life with a set of maps or temporal templates to guide us. Our senses are primed to notice anything that refers to one of our templates so that we can give it more attention when noticed. We already know that what we pay attention to e-x-p-a-n-d-s, that is we get more of it.

It is a very clever biopsychological system with a major upside and a major downside. Let us deal with the upside first. The memories of the future do not have to be realistic or sensible! They are a memory-resident programme that matches for similarity or dissimilarity: is this experience like or unlike one of my templates? Where there is a match, we run the scenario programme to explore the possibilities further.

Dream your wildest dreams, Cinderella, and you may yet go to the ball.

What does this mean? It means that it pays to dream. The more scenarios you have stored in your memory, the more opportunities you will notice for growth, expansion and life to the full.

The mind does not need an exact match, it merely needs some assurance that we are on the right lines. So you can dream outrageous dreams, believe the impossible, and fantasize your ideal life and then your system is set to try and achieve this for you!

The downside? The downside takes us back to our thought-bubbles. If you *do not* run multiple and diverse scenarios, your system has no point of reference. This means that all manner of opportunities will cross your path and you will not notice them. You will get locked in your thought-bubbles and join the 'it doesn't happen to me/if only . . .' brigade rather than the 'what if . . .?' brigade. Which would you prefer?

All this means that Ingvar's work is justification for hopeful romantics, dreamers and poets everywhere. Here is a quote adapted from Goethe which seems to be in alignment with Ingvar's research:

If you don't dream, when opportunity knocks at your door, you won't hear it. You'll be in the back garden, fast asleep, oblivious.

Until one is committed, there is hesitancy, the chance to draw back, always ineffectiveness. Concerning all acts of initiative (and creation), there is one elementary truth, the ignorance of which kills countless ideas and splendid plans; that the moment one definitely commits oneself, then providence moves too.

All sorts of things occur to help one that would never otherwise have occurred. A whole stream of event issues from the decision, raising in one's favour all manner of unforseen incidents and meetings and material assistance which no man could have dreamed would have come his way.

'Whatever you can do or dream you can, begin it. Boldness has genius, power and magic in it. Begin it now.' Goethe

Whatever you can do or dream you can, begin it. Boldness has genius, power and magic in it. Begin it now.

Where does this leave us in the model? Well, I am sure you can perceive the importance of helping your group build future scenarios of how they could apply the learning from your event. If they go beyond action planning, and instead visit some of their potential futures, they will have a far more compelling vision of the possibilities that lay before them.

In the workshop you will need to put some time aside for the learners to visit their likely (and not so likely) futures to notice what cues their environment will give them for making new choices. In practice, I usually have included this as the conclusion to the Go-Again phase exercise – the review concert. This is because they are already relaxed and in an ideal state of mind to use their imagination to explore alternative realities. We are the choices we make.

The key benefit of this scenario planning is that you will *naturally* carry over your learning into the world of everyday life when the scenario begins to play itself out. This means that training really does work, and that it becomes an excellent investment.

BEYOND ACTION PLANNING

Action planning usually asks us, 'What shall we do as a result of this learning?' What I am suggesting is similar yet subtly different. I am asking, 'In what forthcoming contexts could I see myself using this skill?' This puts the action in *context*, in *time* and in *reality*. I fully accept that this can and does happen during action planning, however, here it is a *deliberate* pre-setting of our attention, a loading of our intention, to be prepared for the *cues* our real-life situations are likely to give.

Assertiveness training works well as an example of this. In assertiveness training you explore your view of yourself and of others, and the rights you give each other. You learn to say 'no' and you examine what the triggers are that set you off on the pathway of non-assertive behaviours. On an excellent programme, the facilitator will then remind you that those very triggers that led to non-assertive behaviours will be your future signposts to an alternative choice of path. Next time someone talks to you in 'that tone of voice',

Skills Transfer

Mental rehearsal in the form of scenario planning *naturally* becomes our work experience, making training an excellent investment.

instead of cowering or exploding, you can choose the new skills you practised on the programme.

The habit of review

Out of sight – out of mind. If we want insight on a daily basis we can achieve this by keeping key learning in sight and in mind. There are so many easy ways to do this. Perhaps the deciding factor for ongoing success is whether or not you will make it a habitual part of your day. Here are two ways to help this.

It is usually true that 'out of sight' means 'out of mind' . . .

Placing our history and learning on the walls is a visually powerful way of keeping what is important in-sight, in-mind.

THE LEARNING WALL

History is full of examples of teaching walls. The Bayeux Tapestry, cave paintings, friezes on the walls of temples and palaces throughout the ancient world and the coded messages of graffiti artists in the modern world. These all represent an important way of keeping a key message in sight, in mind. Many of us decorate our walls with memories or visions of what it important to us.

This has a surprisingly positive impact on the memory, especially if it is a growing artistic project. This is because the memory works well with locations (visual/spatial intelligence). A nurse friend of mine revised for her exams by placing memory cues all around her house whilst revising. In the written exam she was able to visit the comforting familiarity of her home, and there the information presented itself to her by association with her familiar household objects and locations. The Roman room system works on this principle. This is where the Romans would memorize vast amounts of information by associating the unfamiliar with familiar locations on a frequent journey or with objects in their home.

The Roman room memory system works by associating each point to be recalled with an already familiar room.

A very powerful way to keep learning in sight and in mind is to dedicate some wall-space to your new learning project. Then build up the map of your new learning sector by sector as you discover your new territory, just like an explorer. You are a pioneer charting strange and wonderful new lands.

If you then get into the habit of daily reviewing your progress on the wall, you will have a head start on maintaining your commitment to the relevance of your new learning. A small change that will make all the difference in the long run is to make sure you *add* something to your wall each day. It does not matter if this is only a tiny addition, but there must be a change if your mind is going to preclude the problem of taking the familiar for granted. As I said at the beginning, Accelerated Learning is a lifestyle. If we only were to make little changes in our relationships each day, adding something special each and every day, we would get to the point where we would not take each other for granted. Joy.

Another way to keep the wall fresh is to move parts of your growing map of your new world around.

Learning is a lifestyle. Making tiny incremental improvements each day leads to joy; the joy of learning and *joie de vivre!*

REVIEW TIME

The second way to build the healthy habit of review is to have a review time and a review system. If you are ready, willing and able to set a specific time aside each day for review you will give your brain a clear message that learning and memory are key imperatives for you. Both are life skills and will improve the quality (and maybe quantity) of your life. Back this up with the following system, and it will be easier.

There is a rhythm to our review cycles of memory. Reviewing in the first 5–10 minutes after a significant discovery, then within the first hour, the next day, the next week, after a month and after three months. This way the precious learning will stay in-sight, in-mind.

Once you are in the habit of Mind Mapping, it is very simple to keep a folder of your maps that are 'under review'. You know the rhythm now: review in the first 5–10 minutes after recording information on your map. Review again briefly within the first hour. The next day. After a week. After a month. Finally, at the three-month stage, if you are content that you have mastered the information. If not, just put it back in the system for further review and development.

Most of my maps are on A4 paper. I have built a review system based around an A4 ring binder. Into this I put two sets of dividers. The first set is January to December. The second set is 1–31.

Say that today's date is 21st August. The folder will be set up at this specific point in time with dividers dated 21–31 behind the August tab and dividers 1–20 behind next month's (September's) tab. If I have a Mind Map that I have created today it will get filed today behind the 21 August partition.

I will often put a box on the back of the map with the dates for review on it and a tick column when the review is completed at each stage. On the back of today's map there will be a section for 5–10 minutes and 60 minutes. After these reviews, the map will be moved to wait behind the 22 divider, ready for tomorrow's review. After tomorrow it will be filed behind the 28 divider, since that is the date of the week's review. After 28 August, the map will be filed in September's section behind the 18 divider for the month's review. Finally it will move into the November section for review around 21 November. Whilst I strictly work out 28 days from the start day for my month's review, I just use the same date three months on from the start for my final review. The map can then be archived.

Only 24 minutes review time over three months gives a huge return on investment.

How long should you review at each session? I suggest merely four minutes. This means 24 minutes over the three months to memorize your learning. A small investment with a great return. Alternatively, you may prefer to use a more active review throughout *some* of the review periods. By this I mean a re-sketching of your learning from memory and then a comparison with the original to see what really has gone in. This will take more time but is *always* worth it for important material.

Engage is the phase where we *make it so!* We make our commitment to the future.

Mindset – *make ready!*

Combining the wall, the system and the timing is a chord of three strands that is not easily broken and is an excellent habit.

Becoming engaged

I think it is time we became engaged, don't you? Let us work together through the M.E.S.S.A.G.E.™ Model and see what action steps you could take. For each and every action step that appeals to you, I would ask you to pause, visit your future, and find a specific example of an instance where you could apply this in your currently expected future. Make a commitment.

I have deliberately kept this short to preclude too much material and duplication. If you are ready for very detailed, step-by-step exploration of the complete model, please go to Appendix B and work through our professional criteria. The following is to whet your appetite and to make sure that you really are installing some magical memories of the future.

MINDSET AND MINDSETTING

○ How could you redesign your joining instructions to be more like marketing materials to attract someone to an adventurous and exciting vacation?
○ How could you increase the energy of your pre-course contact?
○ How could you revolutionize the layout of your training venue to give a fresh and invigorating message that this is different, special and that the learners know they are valued by you?
○ Prepare a music list to add sonic punctuation to your learning points and transitions. What headings work best for you? Choose alternatives for each key point just in case you entrain an inappropriate response!

Entrance – *make sense!*

ENTRANCE

○ How will you make the BIG picture overview compelling, exciting, comprehensive and motivating?

○ How will you create sensory enrichment of every key idea you wish to convey? You are the director. You are the producer. You are the talent (alongside your learners, yet you will lead until they realize what a vital starring role they play). You are the scriptwriter, the one who comes up with the screenplay. Be creative!

○ What activity could you set the group that would build their confidence as a team of group learners?

SWITCH OWNERSHIP

○ How could you orchestrate an activity or two that would ensure every intelligence had to be applied? Remember the list of verbs I asked you to generate earlier. Use them as cues for your ideas and design.

○ How can you ensure that this set of activities is learner driven?

○ How will you recognize what intelligences are being used?

Switch OwNership – *make it intelligible!*

STORE

○ How will you identify the 10 per cent key subject matter? Having this clear in your own mind will help you steer the group if they get sidetracked.

○ What artistic and training resources could you provide in the room to make visual representations of the key points more satisfying and aesthetically rich?

○ How could you use the 'vowels of memory' to help during the Store phase? Reminder: **a**ssociation, **e**mphasis (especially with

Store – *make it stick!*

humour), **i**magination (for example, memory stories), **o**rder (key sequences and priorities, plus the hierarchies of ideas) and the **u**nusual.

ACT

Act – *make it show!*

○ How could you design a connecting grid game?
○ How can you prepare yourself to umpire a team challenge?
○ Visit a toy shop and see what other commercially available family games could be adapted to demonstrate competence and build confidence.

GO-AGAIN

Go-Again – *make it flow!*

○ What pieces of music around the 60 beats per minute tempo will you choose? (Have a selection of at least three.)
○ Do you have a metronome or will you buy or borrow one to practice with? Will you practice emphasizing the beat?
○ What have been the key learning milestones of your life's learning journey? Build these into a sequential story and read it out loud to yourself, blending your voice in time with the background music.

ENGAGE

Engage – *make it so!*

○ Take some time out where you will not be interrupted. Deeply relax and then review your recollections from this learning. Let your mind dream away forwards in time. Notice what opportunities to use these ideas emerge from your imagination.
○ Buy a beautiful notebook to make into your transformational learning journal into life.
○ How will you ascertain the learners' leaving state at the close of the direct portion of your training and development intervention?

○ Which wall will become your learning wall?

○ How will you implement your own review schedule and help your learners manage their post-programme review?

In the suggested action steps above I asked you how you might ascertain the final state of the learners at the close of the direct portion of your training. This is relatively simple, a way of finding out 'Where are we now?' Sometimes I just toss a soft ball around the group and ask them for one sentence or a one word summary of how they feel about their learning at the close of this part of the programme.

If you have time, a very rewarding way to handle this 'Where are we now?' activity is to ask them to choose a poem, a video clip, or a song that summarizes their learning. This then becomes a very powerful associative mechanism for them to anchor their experience and to articulate their experience for the benefit of others. It works particularly well as closure for longer programmes.

Follow-through, validation and evaluation

Whilst I will not go into detail on these headings in this work, they are very important. Particularly powerful is *your* follow-through of the review schedule. There will be many ways in which you can keep in contact with your learners after the direct portion of the programme. If you can orchestrate your follow-through system so that you send your learners something of value after one week, one month and three months, you will really help them realize that the learning is significant. It is also very easy to send them a 'thank you' card that's waiting for them the day after the programme. If your intentions are in their best interest, this will be well received.

Your own 'follow-through' is very important for helping learners keep their investment in-sight, in-mind.

Delegates can write a letter to themselves to remind them of their learning.

Many programmes use the method of delegates writing a letter to themselves to be sent out by the trainer at a random or pre-arranged date. One very special friend of mine got her letter to herself a year after her programme, and it had a hugely beneficial impact. Never forget a learner and never let a learner forget you!

In terms of evaluation, I am not in the habit of handing out 'happy' sheets. I seriously doubt the accuracy of their content and I resent the interruption they represent to the flow of the learning. I recognize their positive intention, but would prefer that learners had a chance to try out their learning and to incubate their knowledge. Providing a stamped addressed envelope is a more effective way of getting valuable evaluation feedback. Let the learners 'sleep on it'.

Validation is another matter. In a time of products and services being over-sold, it is very important that we work towards validating our claims for success. This is expensive and often remains undone, but I would argue that this would be something very valuable to budget for in your training investment and expenditure. It will help you market the training function with integrity.

Summary

The Engage phase is a new beginning. As Covey has said, 'Begin with the end in mind,' so also we can now say, 'End with the beginning in mind.' Learning and development never become common practice unless we create a compelling vision of how we may personally apply our new discoveries. We must create all-consuming memories of the future that continually call to us to realize them in our day-to-day experience. So our 'end' is to consider where each new discovery may 'begin' its application in our daily lives.

Part of this process of envisioning and engaging the future is to literally imagine what it will be like to apply our learning. Another part of this process is to keep the learning in-sight, in-mind by having systems of review to keep them as living daily discoveries. This can be achieved through the use of diary systems, and by the judicious use of wall-space. And the diary system can become even more powerful if combined with the practice of keeping a reflective journal.

THE ART OF REFLECTION

The unexamined life is not worth living.

One of the Greek philosophers said, 'The unexamined life is not worth living.' Accelerated Learning is a lifestyle and if you are to train congruently using Accelerated Training methods you would benefit enormously from practising them yourself on a daily basis. You can then talk from what you know rather than from what you have read. An excellent habit to develop is that of keeping a reflective journal. In this you can store those treasured moments of truth when you have had an insight or an illustration of a key principle. In time, you will become a master storyteller, holding your learners spellbound with your recounting of real examples from your own experience.

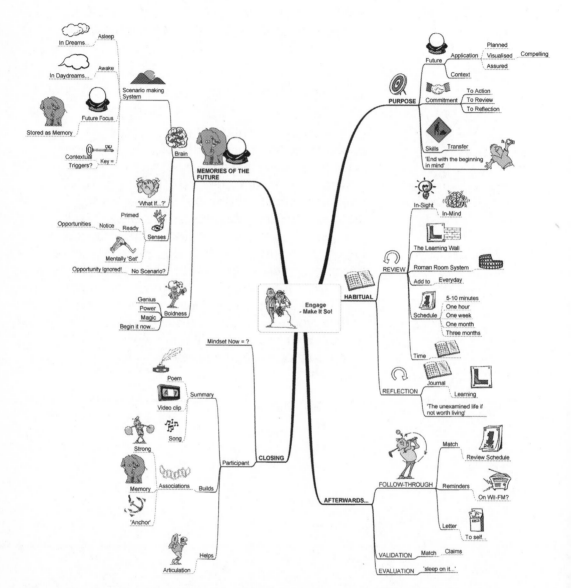

Figure 12 A review Mind Map of the Engage phase

Where Next?

In Appendix B I have included the full set of criteria for the award of the 'Certificate in Accelerated Training Practice'. Whether or not you are interested in pursuing this award with The Registry of Accelerated Trainers, the criteria themselves are very valuable in designing or redesigning your own interventions in detail. If you work through the set systematically, you will have actioned all the key learning points from this publication.

To use the trademark 'Mind Maps®' legally you can seek details from Buzan Centres Ltd: their contact details are in the Appendices. The Registry of Accelerated Trainers, as a body that seeks to represent the interests of Accelerated Trainers, is very keen to be seen as a professional body that behaves ethically in respect to trademarks and copyrights. This is why I have mentioned the Performing Right Society and the issue of the Mind Maps® trademark.

In Closing

You really are the key.

A Vocational Choice

Accelerated Training is a vocation, a calling. It is an enormously satisfying way to give of your time and your energy to others. Every day in every way it gets better and better. If I may add a biographical note? Before becoming a trainer my career history was in 18-month segments, changing jobs over and over again. I have been training now for 21 years. Why the difference? I believe it is because this vocational choice is as satisfying for the trainer as it is for the learner. The discipline is not static; there are new worlds of discovery and opportunity forever opening up as we learn more about the mind and about how human beings can work, learn and live together in synergistic harmony. Together we are more.

I wish you every satisfaction too as you begin to explore the ever more new worlds of Accelerated Training. Enjoy the journey.

REGISTERING YOUR COPY OF THIS BOOK

REGISTER YOUR COPY

As a 'thank you' for buying this book, I would like to make additional materials available periodically to registered readers who have an internet connection. If you visit the registration section of www.learnfast.co.uk and sign in, you will have access to additional files such as software

versions of the summaries in such popular Mind Mapping programmes as Concept Draw Mind Mapper, Mind Genius and Mind Manager. This is one way that we can keep your investment in-sight, in-mind.

© Lex McKee
Designed by Lex McKee: LexStudios@aol.com

Figure 13 Storyboard summary of the M.E.S.S.A.G.E.™ Model

Answers to questions from Act phase

THE CROSSWORD CHALLENGE

	B	R	O	A	D	C	A	S	T	I	N	G						
	B			I			H					L						
	A			M		M	N	E	M	O	N	I	C	S	I			
	I			E			T					N						
	N			N				A	T	T	R	A	C	T	O	R	S	
	B			S								U						V
	R		I	S	L	A	N	D				I						I
	E			O					M	I	N	U	T	E	S			S
	A		C	O	N	F	I	D	E	N	C	E		N		T		U
	K		W		N					T		I				A		
			N		T					R		R	E	C	A	L	L	
			E		P	E	R	I	P	H	E	R	A	L				
N	A	T	U	R	A	L		A				P						
			S			C		I		E	X	P	A	N	D	S		
			H			O		N		R								
			W	I	I	F	M		M		I	N	S	I	G	H	T	
			P			P			E		O							
			E			N				N	O	S	E	B	R	A	I	N
	E	X	P	E	C	T	A	T	I	O	N	S		A		L		
			E			L					L		P					
			N									V	H	F				
	D	I	S	T	R	A	C	T	O	R	S			A				
			E															

THE WORD GRID CHALLENGE

Which 'A' is the communication that Accelerated Trainers use?	ADVANCED
Which 'B' can Accelerated Trainers use to enhance learning?	BRAIN BREAKS
Which 'C' can improve your memory recall by 50 per cent?	COLOUR
Which 'D' can be emphasized through shading?	DIMENSION
Which 'E' represents the last part of the M.E.S.S.A.G.E.™ model of Accelerated Training?	ENGAGE
Which 'F' would we do well to transform into benefits?	FEATURES
Which 'G' is a learning behaviour demonstrated by blue tits, but not by robins?	GROUP
Which 'H' is an activity that will serve us well if under the physical intelligence area?	HANDS-ON
Which 'I' is the intelligence switched on when you ask people to discuss a point of view?	INTERPERSONAL
Which 'L' type recall is found in the rhinencephalon?	LONG-TERM
Which 'M' is the foundation of the M.E.S.S.A.G.E.™ model of Accelerated Training?	MINDSET or MINDSETTING
Which 'N' is a key preference of mathematical-logical intelligence?	NUMBERS or NUMERACY
Which 'O' is beneficial if used for the centre of a mind map?	OPEN
Which 'P' launches our P.O.W.E.R.F.U.L. mnemonic?	POSITIVE
Which 'R' relates to this sequence: 5–10; 60; 24; 7; 31; 93?	REVIEW
Which 'S' belongs to learners in the M.E.S.S.A.G.E.™ model of Accelerated Training?	SWITCHING OWNERSHIP
Which 'T' is a wave useful for deep integration?	THETA
Which 'U' is a key point to do with lines and words on a Mind Map?	UNDERLINING
Which 'V' in general are more effective, the larger and more colourful we make them?	VISUALS
Which 'W' describes WIIFM and VHF?	WAVELENGTHS

Professional criteria: The elements of competence for the award, `Certificate in Accelerated Training Practice'

Unit 1: Prepare and deliver training in full M.E.S.S.A.G.E.™ model Accelerated Learning format

Element	Performance criteria	Range
Mindset/ting		
1.1 Trainer communicates in advance with course participants – with the intention throughout the mindset/ting phase of `making ready'. *Options: further impact may be gained by maintaining a preview schedule of contact with the learner. Material may be sent as much as three months in advance. Imagination is the key – think of how you would attract someone to a*	1.1.1 Prepares and sends welcome pack.	Welcome pack can include: • welcoming letter • details of venue and session timings • participant resources • course overview • learning map of key points • learner success testimonials • introduction to Accelerated Learning • introductory preview cassette • list of suitable pre-course reading • pre-course questionnaires and assessments.

Element	Performance criteria	Range
Mindset/ting (*continued*) *holiday resort - send a colourful and compelling brochure, a postcard or a video. Whilst this degree of interaction is not required for the award, experimentation with the power of this preview technique is recommended in the strongest possible terms and may obtain a distinction.* *Remember that there are different energy levels of contact – face to face being more energetic than e-mail.*		Claims for Accelerated Learning successes to be supported by adequate proof such as audit figures and testimonials
	1.1.2 Formats pack to: • facilitate raising of realistic expectations • begin learning process • stimulate positive interest • introduce Accelerated Learning concepts.	A preview M.E.S.S.A.G.E.™ recording will be regarded as sufficient introduction to Accelerated Learning concepts.
	1.1.3 Provides option of pre-course support and coaching.	Pre-course support may take the form of a contact telephone number or address for questions and concerns.
1.2 Trainer establishes a welcoming environment to promote a continuing state of relaxed awareness amongst the trainees. *(Recommended threefold strategy to relax mind, body and spirit/emotions:* *mind – using the park/dustbin/safe method;* *body – using Romen progressive relaxation;* *spirit/emotions – using Sedona method of questioning for releasing. (Could you? Would you? When?))*	1.2.1 Prepares room layout to encourage positive expectation of safe involvement in learning experience.	Layout to include: • space for activities • non-hierarchical seating • provision for adequate ventilation • provision for temperature control • attention to natural light sources • suitable positioning for peripherals • trainer positioned for maximum eye-contact.
	1.2.2 Prepares and positions peripherals to achieve maximum effect.	Peripheral artwork to include: • positive personal affirmations • affirmations that learning is easy, enjoyable, effective and important • lesson-specific peripherals • positions ready for learners' work. Peripherals should be changed frequently.
	1.2.3 Displays attractive and topical welcome poster.	Welcome poster should: • spell participants' names correctly • use appropriate form of name • carry a topical or seasonal theme • use a minimum of three colours • use dimension • be effectively positioned.
	1.2.4 Utilizes music appropriately. *Sonic entrainment – encouraging a 'frequency following' or 'rhythmic response' through the use of music.*	Music is used: • sporadically • to emphasise transitions, such as entrances and exits • to energize group • to aid relaxation and review • to change state during breaks • to facilitate rhythmic learning • to empower imagery and visualization • to emphasize learning points.
	1.2.5 Makes use of props to enhance positive expectation of learning.	Props may include: • floral displays • physical representations of learning points, for example models.

Element	Performance criteria	Range
Mindset/ting (*continued*)		
	1.2.6 Portrays a positive self-image to encourage similar state in participants. *Personal entrainment – encouraging a 'frequency following' or 'rhythmic response' through the use of body language, non-verbal communication, linguistic patterns, individual feedback and a positive personal internal mindset.*	Positive communication to include: • use of multi-sensory language • non-verbal and verbal suggestions of permission to play, experiment and make mistakes • appropriate use of eye-contact, humour, smiling and participants' names • appropriate use of enthusiasm • sensory acuity and flexibility of behaviour to ensure rapport • positive expectations of success.
1.3 Trainer connects with participants' starting position.	1.3.1 Meets participants where they are by: • eliciting their names • eliciting their roles • eliciting what was on their minds as they came to the seminar. *May be combined with 1.3.2.*	Trainer to lead first.
	1.3.2 Connects by voicing expectations and concerns – for example WIIFM, park, dustbin and safe exercises.	Trainer to lead first. Expectations and concerns collected on 'T' column, and reviewed at close of training.
	1.3.3 Sets parameters for training by soliciting roles and principles and, where necessary, augmenting these to make sure the range statement is adhered to. Ideally there will be a recorded three-way contract between learners, facilitator and the organization with clear expectations and responsibilities for each party.	Suggested roles to include: • host organization's responsibility to provide resources and support, and to receive feedback • participants' responsibility to own their learning, bring their experience, be fully involved, develop teamwork, develop independence and ask questions • trainer's responsibility to provide structure, materials, activities, theories and answers to questions, and to facilitate success. Suggested principles to include: • keeping to agreed start and finish times • aspects of health and safety, plus administration • make mistakes • ask questions via the trainer.
1.4 Trainer facilitates learners' setting of well-formed outcomes thereby eliciting their desired state as a result of applying the training. *Development note: training in neurolinguistic programming will be a useful adjunct to this course of study.*	1.4.1 Outcomes match and meet the 'P.O.W.E.R.F.U.L.' criteria Definitions for P.O.W.E.R.F.U.L.: • **P**ositive: framed in terms of what is desired, not what is to be avoided; 'towards' a goal as opposed to 'away from' it. • **O**wned: that is purely under the control of the goal setter; not reliant on another's change of mind. • **W**IIFM: can articulate the key benefits of achieving the goal and what the achievement will do for you	Due to time restrictions, it may not be appropriate to go systematically and explicitly through all these evidence criteria, so the trainer being assessed should show evidence of well-formed questions to facilitate clarification of learners' outcomes. These questions will be based on a neurolinguistic programme, meta model approach to the structure of language. Clearly then, the Accelerated Trainer should be familiar with the structure and application of the meta model.

Element	Performance criteria		Range
Mindset/ting (*continued*)			
		• **E**videnced: articulated sensory cues that will be markers on the journey to attaining the goal • **R**esourced: able to list the time, personal, and material resources necessary • **F**aith-filled: stated in an 'as if now' format • **U**nique: a simple goal as opposed to a cluster of targets • **L**iving: visited on a daily basis to keep the goal vivid.	
Entrance			
1.5	Trainer shares the big picture – with the intention throughout of helping *fresh* material literally '*make sense'*.	1.5.1	Big picture is comprehensively covered.	Big picture to include: • getting to know each other • clearing our minds for learning • frequent breaks • learning with Accelerated Learning, using: — music — co-operative tasks — imagery — games and activities — multi-sensory approach — role-plays in pairs • overview of subject area • creating personal progress plan • looking back and reflecting.
		1.5.2	Conveyance of big picture to be at least auditory and visual.	Visual aspects to use: • minimum of three colours • dimension. Auditory aspects to use: • good variety of tone • appropriate volume • appropriate explanation of terminology • jigsaw metaphor at least once during course.
1.6	Trainer facilitates and manages a team activity to emphasize team learning and independence from the trainer.	1.6.1	Introduce team learner-centred activity in such a way as to clearly communicate a message of learner self-sufficiency and teamwork.	Team tasks to include: • learning style evaluation • group learning map • artistic activities — expressive — interpretive. Trainer should give non-verbal reinforcement of learner independence by leaving the room at this stage.
1.7	Trainer conducts the lesson stage of the learning event using a range of multi-sensory interventions to engage all learning input preferences.	1.7.1	Provides big picture overview of lesson content and procedure.	Overview to include: • only subject-relevant material • visual representation of overview using a minimum of three colours and dimension.
		1.7.2	Provides linear formatted objectives for lesson part of seminar.	Objectives to be formatted in behavioural terms with active verbs.

Element	Performance criteria	Range
Entrance (*continued*)	1.7.3 Uses 'multiple chance learning' methods to input lesson content, using diversity to augment the multi-sensory approach (compare with the impact of environmental diversity on synaptic enrichment).	Methods of delivery to include: • imagery • mini-lecturettes • audio-visual presentations, for example, booklet and cassette • metaphors • role plays • co-operative learning tasks • peripheral support • intermissions and breaks as part of the strategy (maximizing primacy and recency).
Switch OwNership 1.8 Trainer conducts the switch ownership phase of the learning event by arranging activations that will sequence through the seven intelligences originally proposed by Howard Gardner, thus allowing learners to personalize the learning using their own unique blends of Intelligences, literally '*making it intelligible*'.	1.8.1 Follows entrance of material with appropriate activations to 'switch-on' the following intelligences: • mathematical/logical • linguistic • visual/spatial • physical • interpersonal • intrapersonal • musical.	Activations ideally should be chosen so that more than one specific intelligence at a time is encouraged. This will help maximize the impact whilst minimizing the investment of time.
	1.8.2 Maintains a non-directive approach as far as content goes, since learners should have an adequate grasp of the concepts by now (this is the phase where they can now make the learning their own). Trainer may direct process if the group appears to be meandering.	In practice, it is also acceptable to fuse the entrance and switch ownership phases together ('in phase') where it makes sense that the learners can easily move from grasping new information (entrance) through to deep processing of the material (switch ownership). Tony Buzan's Mind Mapping is an excellent activity that can bridge the entrance, switch ownership, and store phases of the model; an elegant use of resources. For this reason, trainers should be adept at Mind Mapping and be able to articulate all its key principles.
Store 1.9 Trainer facilitates the storage of the mastered material, '*making it stick*'.	1.9.1 Emphasis is on editing the material to represent only the 10 per cent key memory triggers.	Storage techniques to include: • Mind Mapping as the tool of choice • memory flash-cards • team mnemonics and acrostics • raps • T-shirts • drama activities.
Act 1.10 Trainer hosts the act phase of the model supporting the staging of a 'game show' or	1.10.1 Ensures that any questions used fairly cover the material realistically mastered during	Act phase techniques to include, over a period of time: • game shows, such as word grids

Element	Performance criteria	Range
Act (*continued*) dramatic performance demonstration of the material learned, making the learning 'show' for all to see.	entrance, switch ownership, and store phases. 1.10.2 Arbitrates any disputes in any team challenge style 'game show'.	• team challenge activities where the learners are responsible for generating the questions • dramatic presentations of material learned and reframed in the learners' own terms.
Go-Again		
1.11 Trainer orchestrates a musical review of the learning journey (known as the 'review concert' or 'passive concert' and grounded in the work of Georgi Lozanov) with the intent that the known material becomes assimilated at such a deep level that it is acted upon as 'second nature', hence 'Make it flow!' This is similar to the 'flow' state experienced by athletes.	1.11.1 Uses multi-sensory descriptions.	
	1.11.2 Voice used as an 'instrument' in the ensemble, matching the style and pace of the music.	Voice blends to such an extent that the attention of the audience's conscious minds shifts to the rhythm, tempo and style of the music.
	1.11.3 Chooses music that is most likely to entrain a brain wave state where theta waves are likely to dominate (the brain waves most strongly associated with reverie and deep assimilation, as well as unconscious learning and competence).	Choice of music includes most usually the *largo* movements of baroque compositions (for example Vivaldi, Handel, Bach or Telemann). If alternatives, such as Vangelis or Enya, are used, use a metronome to confirm the 60 bpm associated with theta entrainment. A relaxed delegate's breathing rhythm may also be paced for group entrainment.
	1.11.4 Comprehensive coverage of all key learning milestones along the journey.	Comprehensive coverage in logical sequence to facilitate the left hemisphere's preference for order.
	1.11.5 Positive use of suggestion to replace barriers to learning and integration with confident competence and self-assurance.	Suggestion focuses on learner empowerment and independence rather than any sense of psychological manipulation or dependency on trainer activities.
Engage		
1.12 Trainer encourages the habitual practice of the optimum review schedule. All activities during this phase have the intention of making application of the learning in the rest of the participant's experience a natural consequence; hence 'Make it so!'	1.12.1 Highlights the key temporal review markers for transferring short-term memory material to long-term: • within the first hour (5–10 minutes and 60 minutes) • after one day • after one week • after one month • after three months (93 days).	Any review system should facilitate the ease of implementing this strict review schedule (memory jogger: 'out-of-sight, out-of- mind; in-sight, in-mind').
	1.12.2 Articulates the destructive influence of interruptions to review during the first hour post-programme.	Hint: highlight the interference of mobile phones and message boards – the two major negators of the clearing-the-mind-for learning.
1.13 Trainer encourages the habitual practice of reflection.	1.13.1 Highlights the use of some reflection tool such as a learning journal or regular meetings with a mentor or 'study buddy'.	

Element	Performance criteria	Range
Engage (*continued*)		
1.14 Trainer encourages the habitual construction of 'memories of the future' – multiple scenario exploration.	1.14.1 Articulates the perceptual impact of running multiple possible future scenarios on the performance of the learners' sensory awareness.	Compare with the work of David Ingvar of the University of Lund, Sweden.
1.15 Trainer closes the training event by ascertaining the leaving state of participants.	1.15.1 Reviews the expectations and concerns 'T' column exercise.	
	1.15.2 Solicits the 'What went well?' and 'What could have been better?' for each participant.	Journal should be kept of actioned suggested improvements.
	1.15.3 Ends on a positive note by asking participants to summarize learning event in one word or short phrase.	Trainers should 'catch themselves doing something right' and reward themselves accordingly.
1.16 Trainer carries out post-course follow-up, evaluation and validation.	1.16.1 Follows-up all course participants within three weeks.	Follow-up may take the form of face-to-face review meeting, telephone call or letter.
	1.16.2 Executes formal evaluation procedures.	Results to be collated, analysed and responded to.
	1.16.3 Seeks validation of claims of course successes and methodologies and adapts accordingly.	Journal to record changes and observations made; details of research may be counted towards Master of Accelerated Training.

Unit 2: Produce Mind Maps® that conform to Buzan Centres, Ltd standards of the key principles

Element		Performance criteria		Range
2.1	Trainer articulates the key Mind Map® principles.	2.1.1	Paper used is landscape in orientation	Paper sizes recommended are A4 or larger.
	(Mind Maps® is the registered trademark of Buzan Centres, Ltd. This registration mark should be acknowledged with all printed uses of the term 'Mind Maps®	2.1.2	Focal point is central image of appropriate size.	On A4 sheet, image should be about 4 cm × 4 cm.
		2.1.3	Images are used extensively for the centre with the outcome of distinctiveness.	Submitted sample Mind Maps® should demonstrate distinctiveness either through images or imagistic words.
		2.1.4	Central image uses a minimum of three colours.	Complementary colours are recommended.
		2.1.5	Central image has dimension to make it appear to stand out.	Dimension may be demonstrated using shading or 3D effects.
		2.1.6	Main themes radiate out on branches attached to the central image.	
		2.1.7	Main themes are represented by a single word or image.	Main themes are capitalized and are distinguishable from other themes by use of colour or alternative font styles.
		2.1.8	Words or images are of key nature only.	Key words are nouns or active verbs; adjectives or adverbs should be justified by candidate.
		2.1.9	Words are printed.	Printed and capitalized near the centre.
		2.1.10	Words are always on a line.	Each word touches a line.
		2.1.11	Lines are curved or 'organic'.	By 'organic' we mean soft and curvy, reflecting nature.
		2.1.12	Lines emphasize the length of each word or image – underlining the thought.	
		2.1.13	All lines are connected in linear flow.	Tiny projections are OK if this assists spatial arrangement.
		2.1.14	Lines thicken on approaching the centre.	Connections should be smooth, with no 'twig'-like projections.
		2.1.15	Second, third and subsequent levels of thought are added towards the periphery.	Levels of thought should be distinguishable by font style, size or colour.

Element	Performance criteria	Range
	2.1.16 Arrows, or colours and codes are used to codify and link common areas.	'Commonality' means linked or identical themes, to produce strong associations.
	2.1.17 Emphasis is added using outlining, highlighting or use of emboldened text.	Outlining may be explicit or implicit (using highlighting or shading).
	2.1.18 The mental effect of 'Gestalt' is enhanced by outlining completed areas of the Mind Map.	The outcome is a unique overall shape for each Mind Map to enhance the ease of filing through distinctiveness of shape and form.

APPENDIX C

List of useful resources and contacts

WEBSITES

LearnFast World Ltd   www.learnfast.co.uk

The organization that hosts the Registry of Accelerated Trainers. Provides training and assessment in the M.E.S.S.A.G.E.™ model of Accelerated Training, and all manner of resources to facilitate Accelerated Training. Trial versions of all key Mind Mapping software can be downloaded from this site. You can also register your copy of this book and get support. The site contains a comprehensive reading list for future development.

The Lex Studios Group   www.lexstudios.com

Providers of music and other resources designed to switch on various advanced learning states of mind (mindsetting, entrance, review, Mind Mapping, super memory).

Buzan Centres, Ltd   www.mind-map.com

Buzan Centres are the only company licenced to train trainers to deliver instruction in Mind Mapping. This is the originator of Buzan brain-friendly training.

Performing Right Society   www.prs.co.uk

You can find out details about how to use music legally within the training context.

Lifetools, Ltd   www.lifetools.com

Providers of sound and light entrainment equipment and many other
resources to assist learning and development.

Accelerated Learning Systems, Ltd   www.accelerated-learning-uk.co.uk

The company founded by Colin Rose. Pioneers in applications of Accelerated
Learning for languages.

Providers of Mind Mapping Software in alphabetical order

ConceptDraw Mind Mapper (Apple and PC)   www.conceptdraw.com
MindGenius (PC only)   www.ygnius.com
MindManager (PC only)   www.murge.com

APPENDIX D

Some suggested music

MUSIC FOR ENTRANCES

Artiste	*Track*	*Potential Source*
Julie London	*Fly me to the moon*	The best of Julie London 'The liberty years' Liberty CDP 7 91298 2
Enya	*Book of days*	Shepherd Moons WEA 9031–75572–2
Genesis	*Invisible touch*	Invisible Touch Virgin GEN CD 2
Peter Gabriel	*Sledgehammer*	Shaking the Tree Virgin PGTVD 6
Wagner	*Ride of the Valkyrie*	Classical commercials Hallmark Classics 350462
Handel	*Arrival of the Queen of Sheba*	Any Handel compilation
U2	*Discotheque*	Pop Island CIDU210 524 334–2
Ottmar Liebert	*The night*	Gypsy passion (new Flamenco compilation) NARADA COLLECTION SERIES ND-63931
Yello	*Oh yeah*	Yello 1980–1985 The new mix in one go Vertigo 826 773–2 Q
Marc Antoine	*Sunland*	Madrid GRP Records GRP 99262

MUSIC FOR EXITS

Artiste	Track	Possible source
Beatles	*Hello, goodbye*	The Beatles/1967–1970 EMI Records Ltd 0777 7 97039 20
Mark Knopfler	*Going home*	Local hero
Andrea Bocelli	*Con te partiro*	Romanza Philips 456 456–2
Ella Fitzgerald	*Every time we say goodbye*	The incomparable Ella Polydor 835 610–2

MUSIC FOR TRANSITIONS

Artiste	Track	Possible source
Tchaikovsky	The Nutcracker Suite	Classical commercials Hallmark Classics 350462

MUSIC FOR GROUP ENERGIZING

Artiste	Track	Possible source
The Who	*Pinball wizard*	My generation – the very best of the Who Polydor 533 150–2
Elton John	*Saturday night's alright*	Goodbye yellow brick road This Record Co Ltd 528 159–2
Van Halen	*Jump*	1984 Warner Bros 7599–23985–2
Gipsy Kings	most tracks from	Greatest hits Columbia COL 477242 2
J S Bach	Brandenburg Concertos	in *'Baroque treasuries'* 5 CD set, Laserlight 35 880
Frank Sinatra	For example, *I've got you, under my skin*	My way – the best of Frank Sinatra; Warner Music 9362–46712–2
Handel	*The arrival of the Queen of Sheba*	
Edward Elgar	Pomp and circumstance no 1 Op 39	

MUSIC FOR RELAXATION AND REVIEW, AND REVIEW CONCERTS

Artiste	*Track*	*Possible source*
Eric Satie (Orch. Debussy)	Gymnopedie no 1	Classical commercials Hallmark Classics 350462

This is by far my all time favourite piece for concert reviews.

Vivaldi	*The four seasons*, especially each of the *largo* movements	The four seasons Laserlight 15 656

This is available as part of a very useful baroque collection called 'Baroque treasuries'; a five CD set from Laserlight 35 880. It contains music by Vivaldi, Bach, Handel and Telemann. The only key composer missing would be Corelli.

For a really interesting alternative to straight classical, it is always worth experimenting with the Jacques Loussier
Trio's version of Vivaldi's '*Four seasons*'   TELARC CD-83417
Also listen to his 'Jacques Loussier plays Bach'   TELARC CD-83411

A Virgin records compilation 'Pure Moods' also
has a wealth of mood-creating music   Virgin Records VTCD 28

MUSIC TO CHANGE MINDSET DURING BREAKS

This is one of the 'safest' times to allow participants to put on their own choice of music, hence having a greater stake in the learning experience. For cues to get people to return from breaks, we suggest:

Artiste	*Track*	*Possible source*
Beatles	*Get back*	The Beatles/1967–1970 EMI Records Ltd 0777 7 97039 20
Rossini	*William Tell overture*	101 Famous classical masterpieces Avid Records MAK 101–4

MUSIC TO FACILITATE RHYTHMIC LEARNING

Artiste	*Track*	*Possible source*
Queen	'*We will rock you*'	Queen's greatest hits Vol 1 EMI Records CDP 7 46033 2
Offenbach	*Cancan*	Classical commercials Hallmark Classics 350462

MUSIC TO EMPOWER IMAGERY AND VISUALIZATION

Under this category I would include key tracks for **concert reviews**, as above.

MUSIC TO EMPHASIZE SPECIFIC LEARNING POINTS FROM YOUR KEY PROGRAMMES

This section is absolutely content specific. For example, a customer service programme may use *Keeping the customer satisfied* by Simon and Garfunkel, or *Satisfaction* by the Rolling Stones, to add both humour and a memory anchor.

Further Reading

Accelerated learning and training

Dhority, Lynn (1992), *The ACT Approach – The Use of Suggestion for Integrative Learning*. London: Taylor & Francis.
Lawlor, Michael and Handley Peter (1996), *The Creative Trainer – Holistic facilitation skills for accelerated learning*. London: McGraw-Hill.
Lozanov, Georgi (1992), *Suggestology and Outlines of Suggestopedy*. New York: Taylor & Francis.
Rose, Colin (1985), *Accelerated Learning*. Aylesbury: Accelerated Learning Systems Ltd.

Mental literacy®

Buzan, Tony, and Keene, Raymond (1994), *Buzan's Book of Genius*. London: Hutchinson.
Buzan, Tony (2003), *The Mind Map Book*. London: BBC Consumer Publishing.
Buzan, Tony (2003), *The Speed Reading Book*. London: BBC Consumer Publishing.
Buzan, Tony (2003), *Use Your Memory*. London: BBC Consumer Publishing.
Russell, Peter (1980), *The Brain Book*. New York: Routledge.

Lateral thinking

de Bono, Edward (1990), *Lateral Thinking – A Textbook of Creativity*. London: Penguin.
de Bono, Edward (1993), *Serious Creativity*. London: Harper Collins Publishers
de Bono, Edward (2000), *Six Thinking Hats*. London: Penguin.

Neurolinguistic programming and related fields

James, Tad and Woodsmall, Wyatt (1988) *Time Line Therapy and the Basis of Personality.* Capitola, CA: Meta Publications Inc.

Knight, Sue (1995), *NLP at Work*. London: Nicholas Brealey Publishing.
O'Connor, Joseph and Seymour, John (1993), *Introducing Neuro-Linguistic Programming*. London: Harper Collins.
O'Connor, Joseph and Seymour, John (1994), *Training with NLP – Skills for Trainers, Managers & Comminicators*. London: Harper Collins.

Transactional analysis

Harris, Amy and Harris, Thomas A. (1995), *Staying OK*. Portland, OR: Arrow.
Harris, Thomas A. (1995), *I'm OK, You're OK*. Portland, OR: Arrow.
Hay, Julie (1996), *Transactional Analysis for Trainers*. Watford: Sherwood Publishing.

Excellence and service

Carlzon, Jan (1989), *Moments of Truth*. London: Harper Collins Publishers.

Conflict resolution and assertiveness

Back, Ken and Back, Kate (1999), *Assertiveness at Work*. London: McGraw-Hill.
Cornelius, Helena and Faire, Shoshana (1994), *Everyone Can Win*. London: Simon & Schuster.

Hypnosis

Elman, Dave (1964), *Hypnotherapy*. Haverford, PA: Westwood Publishing Co.
Lankton, Stephen R. and Lankton, Carol H. (1983), *The Answer Within*. New York: Bunner/Mazel Inc.
Rossi, Ernest L. (1993), *The Psychobiology of Mind-Body Healing*. New York: W W Norton.

Reframing

Bandler, Richard and Grinder, John (1984), *Reframing*. Moab, UT: Real People Press.
Frankl, Viktor E. (1997), *Man's Search for Meaning*. London: Simon & Schuster.

Diversity in intelligence

Gardner, Howard (1993), *Frames of Mind – The Theory Of Multiple Intelligences*. New York: Basic Books Inc.

Personal development

Covey, Stephen R. (1989), *The 7 Habits of Highly Effective People*. London: Simon & Schuster.
Covey, Stephen R. (1996), *First Things First*. Upper Saddle River, NJ: Prentice Hall and IBD.
Thomson, Peter (2000), *Secrets of Communication*. London: Simon & Schuster.

Index

Join our email newsletter

Gower is widely recognized as one of the world's leading publishers on management and business practice. Its programmes range from 1000-page handbooks through practical manuals to popular paperbacks. These cover all the main functions of management: human resource development, sales and marketing, project management, finance, etc. Gower also produces training videos and activities manuals on a wide range of management skills.

As our list is constantly developing you may find it difficult to keep abreast of new titles. With this in mind we offer a free email news service, approximately once every two months, which provides a brief overview of the most recent titles and links into our catalogue, should you wish to read more or see sample pages.

To sign up to this service, send your request via email to **info@gowerpub.com.** Please put your email address in the body of the email as confirmation of your agreement to receive information in this way.

GOWER

If you have found this book useful you may be
interested in other titles from Gower

Legendary Away Days:
The Complete Guide to Running Successful Team Events
Karen Cooley and Kirsty McEwan
0 566 08549 6

How to Set Up and Manage a Corporate Learning Centre
Samuel A. Malone
0 566 08532 1

The Handbook of Work Based Learning
Ian Cunningham, Graham Dawes and Ben Bennett
0 566 08541 0

Individual Preferences in e-Learning
Howard Hills
0 566 08456 2

e-HR:
Using Intranets to Improve the Effectiveness of Your
People
Bryan Hopkins and James Markham
0 566 08539 9

The People Measurement Manual:
Measuring Attitudes, Behaviours and Beliefs in Your
Organization
David Wealleans
0 566 08380 9

For further information on these and all our titles visit our
website – www.gowerpub.com
All online orders receive a discount

GOWER